WALKING WITH THE WISE

GOD'S PLAN FOR PARENTS AND TEENS

BENNY AND SHEREE PHILLIPS

SERIES EDITOR: GREG SOMERVILLE

PEOPLE OF DESTINY
INTERNATIONAL

People of Destiny International serves a growing network
of local churches in the United States and abroad.
For information about the ministry or for permission
to reproduce portions of this book, contact:

People of Destiny International
7881 Beechcraft Avenue, Suite B
Gaithersburg, MD 20879

Authors: Benny and Sheree Phillips
Cover design by Gallison Design
Book layout by Martin Stanley

ISBN 1-881039-04-8

Printed in the United States of America

ACKNOWLEDGMENTS

We are very grateful to the following individuals for your help in making this project possible:

Greg Somerville—For your valuable contributions as an editor and your obvious heart for the next generation.

Larry and Doris, Mark and Marie—For walking with us as fellow parents for over a decade, helping to shape our vision and feed our faith for parenting in the teen years.

Our wonderful friends at Fairfax Covenant Church—For your prayers, encouragement, and support during the busy weeks of writing.

The many great teens in People of Destiny's related churches who are radical followers of Jesus Christ—For becoming living examples of the principles in this book. You give us faith for the next generation!

And to Josh and Jaime—For your helpful suggestions about the manuscript; your help with meals and younger siblings during writing sessions; your friendship; and—most important—for making parenting teens more fun and fulfilling than we ever imagined. We love you!

CONTENTS

HOW TO USE THIS BOOK

Walking With The Wise is one of a series of books published by People of Destiny International to encourage and equip Christians. The series is the logical outgrowth of four deeply-held convictions:

■ The Bible is our infallible standard for faith, doctrine, and practice. Those who resist its authority will be blown off course by their own feelings and cultural trends.

■ Knowledge without application is lifeless. In order to be transformed, we must apply and practice the truth of God's Word in daily life.

■ Application of these principles is impossible apart from the Holy Spirit. While we must participate in change, he is the source of our power.

■ The church is God's intended context for change. God never intended for us to live isolated from or independent of other Christians. Through committed participation in the local church, we find instruction, encouragement, correction, and opportunities to press on toward maturity in Christ.

Whereas other titles in the series are equally good for individual or group study, *Walking With The Wise* is designed specifically for *parents to use with their own teens*. We recommend that parent(s) and teen first read the material separately—if possible, have separate copies. Then use the questions at the end of each study, as well as any questions of your own, to explore the material together.

Both parents are welcome to participate. If only one parent is going to be involved, then we encourage fathers to pair up with sons and mothers with daughters. If you are a single parent and don't have that option, trust God to make your involvement just as significant.

You won't have to go beyond Study One to see there's plenty here to keep you busy! Don't feel you have to complete every question or look up every Bible verse. (On the other hand, as with any self-guided study, you will benefit in proportion to the amount of effort you invest.)

Set a pace that allows you both to get the most from the material. A week may be plenty. Perhaps you'll need a month. Whatever rate you choose, be consistent. These aren't just assignments…these are steps toward a rich, rewarding relationship.

—**Greg Somerville,** *Series Editor*

FOREWORD

From your experience, has t...e...e...n become a four-letter word?

Sadly, it has for many parents. Having grown up with the "me-generation" mentality of the '60s and '70s, today's parents want more for their kids than teenage toys and thrills. Yet many feel ill-equipped for the task. Parenting adolescents requires more wisdom and courage than we bargained for!

Author George Barna tells the story of the frog and the kettle of water. If you put a frog in a pot of boiling water, he'll jump out immediately. (Hey, who wouldn't?!) But if you put a frog in a pot of water at room temperature and then slowly heat the water to boiling, the frog stays in the pot until he cooks to death.[1]

Many Christian parents share the same weakness. We want to raise godly children who become difference-makers for Jesus Christ. We don't want them to suffer the painful consequences of adolescent sin like we—or others we know—have. Yet like frogs in a pot, we watch passively as the temperature climbs in our homes.

The heat of adolescence starts early. And subtly. Your 11-year-old starts arguing with your decisions about how he wears his hair or how much time he spends on homework. Your 13-year-old pouts about not being able to go to a dance with a boy she likes at school. Your 15-year-old accuses you of treating him like a little kid because he's not allowed to watch a hot, new movie with some friends. Your 12-year-old lies about how long she spent talking on the telephone.

Incidents like these happen one by one over the years. You've been told they are normal adolescent behavior. But you don't realize that with each such incident the heat has just been turned up a notch.

It's happening in your life, too. Having a teenager is exposing some things you didn't know were there. Things like impatience. Critical attitudes. Fear. A lack of courage to talk about and address tough issues. The desire to maintain peace in the home, even when it means compromising your standards.

Little by little, the temperature is rising. And too few parents realize it until it reaches the boiling point. Your teen yells at you. Lies about where he was. Disobeys a clear rule. Gets into a compromising situation with her boyfriend. Calls you a hypocrite.

How hot is your pot? Are you still at room temperature where things appear to be fine between you and your teen? Has the temperature in your home heated up some, and you're starting to realize it's a bit uncomfortable? Or have you and your teen reached the boiling point of tension, hopelessness, and strife?

We have six children. Two of them are teenagers. Like you, we've made mistakes. In the past few years we've spent many hours crying out to God for help. And we've found it—in the Bible and in the wise counsel of trusted friends. It's our desire to share some of these insights with you so you can turn down the heat and enjoy a wonderfully fulfilling relationship as parents and teens.

By the way, when we chose the title *Walking With the Wise*, we weren't referring to ourselves. We're talking about *you*! You're the wise counselor and friend who can and should be walking with your teen through the joys and challenges of adolescence. And you need to take seriously *your* responsibility to make the relationship a success. Parents contribute to the tension and misunderstandings, too. Yet with a biblical strategy and the humility to admit our mistakes, we can see the parent/teen relationship strengthen—not weaken—during the teenage years.

Though grammatically we will refer to parents in the plural, we have written this book just as much for those heroic single moms and dads who are working hard to raise children alone. (We're privileged to know many!) We also recognize that a growing number of Christian families are blended with children from previous marriages. Your unique challenges as a family don't have to keep your teen from becoming all he or she can be in God. We hope you'll find help and encouragement in these pages.

We want to say up front that we aren't writing this book as "experts." We're just parents who passionately desire that our teens enjoy a vital and growing relationship with God...and with us. In our search for good training materials, though—and we've searched extensively!—we have found very little that consistently upholds the high biblical standards for parents and teens. As grateful as we are for the resources you'll find quoted throughout, we cannot personally endorse each one. (Those which we do recommend are mentioned at the end of several of the studies.)

The stuff you're about to read isn't being widely communicated. Nor is it the trendy new approach to parenting teens. It's simply straight talk from parents who, like you, are caught up in the daily adventure of serving and shaping those budding adults in our homes.

"Teen" doesn't have to be a four-letter word. Parents need not dread these years. God is raising up a generation of young people who are sold out to him! And he's looking for some courageous parents to lead them through the training process.

Parents, let's get *out* of the pot and give ourselves to the task!

—Benny and Sheree Phillips

CAUTION: MYTH EXPLOSION!

BIBLE STUDY   Luke 9:23-25

WARM-UP   For its size, Albania is the most heavily fortified nation on earth. Though only a little bigger than Vermont (11,100 square miles), it boasts 600,000 concrete bunkers—that's one for every 5.6 citizens! All were built after World War II as protection from an attack that never came.

Now for some math: Imagine that Albania decided to demolish all its bunkers. To do so, each citizen would have to contribute two sticks of dynamite. And each stick of dynamite costs the equivalent of $5 in U.S. currency. What would it cost Albania's citizens to blow up these unnecessary bunkers?

(See page 14 for answer)

PERSONAL STUDY   *Teenager.*

Just saying the word almost overloads your brain. For the teen, it brings to mind fun-filled thoughts of driving… parties with friends…more freedoms in dress, make-up, or hairstyle…and relationships with the opposite sex. Most parents, though, feel differently about the teenage years. Driving? *Oh, no!* More freedoms with their appearance? *Just take a look at these old pictures of what some of my "experiments" looked like!* Spending time with someone of the other sex? *Maybe when she's 30!*

We have six children. When they were younger, we got our share of stares and "How in the world do you do it?" comments. Now that our two oldest are teens, people no longer gawk at us as if we were part of a freak show. These days their looks are mostly sympathetic.

An older couple in a restaurant shake their heads knowingly as if to say, "It's okay, you'll live through it… hopefully." A mother walks past with her two toddlers, her quick glance saying, "I'm glad mine are still young." Or we get the "I know just what you're going through" look from parents in the mall whose teen walks sullenly beside them wearing earphones.

Whether you know it or not, teens, there's something about you that can frighten even the strongest and most self-confident adults. Consider the man whose leadership and management skills have gained him respect and promotions on the job. Yet, to avoid another "scene" with his 16-year-old son, this dad reluctantly tosses him the keys to his new car. Or take the woman known among her friends or co-workers for having it together, being decisive and seemingly in charge of her environment. But when it comes to her 13-year-old daughter, this mom is easily manipulated and willing to let her teen decide what's best. At least she's a lot easier to live with that way.

Maybe these stereotypes don't describe your home. But most families (ours included) face a unique set of challenges during the teenage years. We have disagreements. Sometimes make thoughtless or unkind remarks. Disappoint each other. Have questions about what's "too strict." And yet, like you, we desire to see our Christian faith have an impact on all we do. We don't want to be hypocrites who live one way around our church friends and another way behind the closed doors of our home.

And none of us needs to. Our relationship with God holds the solutions to any problems we might have in our relationships with others, especially those we love most— our family. Our Father has a plan, and the rest of this book is devoted to explaining how it works.

But first we need to take a good hard look at this complex individual we call "the teenager."

Think about 2 Peter 1:3-4. God has already given us everything we need to live the right way, the best way...his way!

Who Invented The Teenager?

Imagine life without electricity. No lamps. Refrigerators. Televisions. CD players. Coke machines. Computers. Video games. Or curling irons.

And no pizza. (Really...how would you cook it?) We're all grateful to Thomas Edison and these other inventors who built on his ideas. (Except when it's time to vacuum your room or type a research paper, right?)

Like electricity, everything had a beginning. Someone invented the wheel, discovered antibiotics, and made popcorn for the first time. So what would you say if we told you there was life before "the teenager"?

It's true. Teenagers didn't always exist. They were invented. And quite recently, at that.

You don't believe it? Take a look at *Webster's Dictionary* from half a century ago. In 1934, only the adjective "teen-age" is listed. It was a word used simply to describe someone in a particular stage of life: a "teen-age" girl, as opposed to a "middle-age" man. Not until his third edition in 1961 did Webster list "teenager" as a noun.

This may sound a little picky, but it's not. The point is an important one. By the release of his third edition, young people had become so identified as "teenagers" that Webster needed to give them their own definition.

So what happened during those 27 years to change society's view of adolescents?

Digging deeper: Read Proverbs 4:1-9. Instead of living from party to party during their teens, godly youth will set their hearts on finding wisdom.

Before World War II teens were called "youths." They were also commonly called kids, boys, girls, young men, young women, lads, and even ladies or gentlemen. Though certainly similar to today's teens, these youth were distinct in two important ways.

First, youths understood the importance of preparing for the future. They no longer considered themselves children. They looked forward to adulthood, and got ready for it by learning the responsibilities of providing and caring for a family. Their heroes were presidents, teachers, parents, and scientists.

Second, youths weren't regularly separated from their parents or teachers. Parents took seriously the responsibility to oversee their children's relationships, job training, and education. Even social functions were attended by both youths and adults. Dr. Michael Platt, an author and educator, describes the difference with this pointed remark: "When you saw youths with their parents, they were not pretending to be unrelated to the family."[1]

What a contrast! Few of today's teens are working hard to prepare for the future…they are *partying* hard, squeezing in as much fun as they can before adult responsibilities catch up with them! They have their favorite rock stars and sports heroes, but probably wouldn't be able to name more than a handful of presidents or scientists. And like magnets turned the wrong way, they and their parents seem to force each other in

> ❝ The Teenager is the most free and the least happy of beings…So far as I know, there have never been such youths on earth before. The Teenager is a novelty not only in the history of twentieth century America, but in the history of the human race.[2] ❞
>
> —Dr. Michael Platt

opposite directions. We pray this doesn't describe you, but it sure paints an accurate picture of the average American teen. Even those who claim to be Christians.

---

1 How well do you know your heroes? Draw a line connecting the person on the left with his/her accomplishment on the right.
(Answers are printed upside down at bottom of page.)

Neil Armstrong	A. Botanist, chemist, educator
Harriet Tubman	B. British prime minister
Sir Winston Churchill	C. Founder of Red Cross
Marie Curie	D. First to walk on moon
George Washington Carver	E. Abolitionist
Clara Barton	F. Chemist and physicist

So who invented the teen? No particular person, but rather a society of people. Over time, youths drifted further and further from adults. As they were allowed to spend increasing amounts of unsupervised time with their peers, an entire sub-culture was born with its own styles of dress and music. Cars and movie theaters paved the way for a new thing called "dating." And somehow the idea was born that the teen years were for "having fun," not for preparing for adulthood as their parents and grandparents had done.

> *Today's youth go out into the adult world carrying the values of a misguided adolescence...The message is plain: life is for looks, for fun, for emotional excitement. Duty? Responsibility? Serious mindedness? These are no longer popular notions.[3]*
>
> **—Michael Keating**

Remember Peter Pan? In many ways he became the model for the emerging teen during this time of transition four decades ago. He didn't want to "grow up." Rather, he lived in a fantasy world without any hassles or interference from adults. (Except for Captain Hook, of course, and you know who the villain was!) Pan had respect from his friends, authority, and unsupervised fun, but no real-life responsibilities. He was the forever teen.

How could former generations who helped turn "youths" into "teens" have known that things would get to

Answers: Armstrong (D), Tubman (E), Churchill (B), Curie (F), Carver (A), Barton (C)

Think about Proverbs 15:10. Is it any surprise families have problems when they leave the path of God's plan?

the point they are today? The changes started slowly, and probably seemed harmless at first. No big deal. But little by little we've drifted from God's plan for young men and women. And today numerous families—including many who are actively involved in churches—are at each other's throats. Parents are in pain because their sweet, innocent children have become complaining, argumentative teens who play their music loud and never come out of their rooms—except to go see friends. Teens are confused because they don't think they "measure up" to Dad's and Mom's expectations or because they feel they're still being treated like kids.

And the society around us says this is normal. In fact, if rocker David Crosby's words are any indication, some have actually made it their goal to rip parents and teens apart:

> I figured that the only thing to do was steal their kids. I still think it's the only thing to do. By saying that, I'm not talking about kidnapping. I'm just talking about changing people's value systems, which removes them from their parents' world very effectively.[4]

Digging deeper: Read 1 Timothy 4:12-16. We don't know exactly how old Timothy was, but we know he was young. Does Paul lower his standards for Timothy due to his age?

Our society has deceived us into accepting some very unbiblical assumptions about teens. By and large we've been convinced that every young man and woman—even those who say they know and love Jesus Christ—will inevitably go through certain "normal" phases of adolescent rebellion. Yet this "teens will be teens" attitude is devastating families and churches across America. Such unbiblical expectations are hindering an entire generation of young people from embracing God's call on their lives.

Let others call these phases normal. We're going to call them myths. And in the pages that follow, we intend systematically to detonate each of them.

A Look At The "Lost Generation"

So do we throw away the term "teenager" and start all over? Not a bad idea—but that's really not the problem. Besides, we firmly believe God is raising up a counter-culture of young people with such a radical commitment to Jesus Christ that we stop thinking of "teen" as a four-letter-word.

The potential for today's Christian teen to stand out for God is there. We're meeting more and more such radicals. But let's dig a little deeper to understand today's average

TEN MYTHS ABOUT TEENS AND PARENTS

MYTH #1 Parents and teens aren't able to communicate or agree on anything.

MYTH #2 Teens naturally go through a season of rebellion; the wise parent will give a teen "space" until he/she grows out of it.

MYTH #3 Moodiness, preoccupation with appearance, and peer dependence are unavoidable symptoms of adolescence.

MYTH #4 Parents tend to be too strict; they need to back off from getting overly involved in their teens' decisions.

MYTH #5 Teens learn right and wrong by experimenting; they can't be expected to resist certain temptations.

MYTH #6 Dating helps teens learn to relate in a healthy way to the opposite sex.

MYTH #7 Professionally trained adults are better equipped than parents to teach teens what they need to know during these years.

MYTH #8 Teens who become spiritually apathetic and lose interest in the church will eventually turn out okay, especially if their parents don't overreact.

MYTH #9 Teens must develop positive self-esteem by learning to love and accept themselves.

MYTH #10 Teens are too young to be leaders and difference-makers.

teens and the culture that's seeking to shape them.

You've probably heard the term "baby boomer." This is the word used to describe the generation of babies born after World War II. Well, the boomers are parents now. And our children are being called "busters."

In his book, *The Invisible Generation: Baby Busters*, researcher George Barna describes this group of young people born between 1965 and 1983 as:

> ...*a very different breed of Americans* than we have previously witnessed. They were raised differently; they communicate distinctively; their aspirations are unique;...and their numbers position them as a force to be reckoned with.[5]

Barna further describes "busters" as "world-class skeptics...cynical about the future"; "concerned [only] with those issues that affect them personally"; and feeling "estranged from family, from community, from God, and often from self."[6]

Busters are the second largest generation in history, representing more than one-quarter of the U.S. population!

Perhaps you think Barna's descriptions could fit any recent generation of teens. Maybe so. Yet *this* generation surely has its unique problems. Some have called today's youths "Generation X" or "the lost generation." They are wanderers, unsure of who they are or how they can make a mark on society. They have suffered in record numbers from watching their parents hurt each other and eventually divorce. They've spent countless lonely hours after

Think about Matthew 11:28-30. The words of Jesus offer tremendous comfort for a disillusioned generation of youth.

school waiting for Mom and Dad to come home from work. And they have struggled to believe Christianity is real while seeing church leaders fall left and right.

No generation of Americans has seen these once-solid foundations of society—the family and the church—rocked so hard. No wonder they're skeptical and insecure.

---

2 Which of the following are most important to today's teens? Make your picks by ranking them from 1 (most important) to 8 (least important).
(Answers are printed upside down at bottom of page.)

__ Family conflicts

__ Doing well in school

__ Having life goals or purpose

__ Career choice

__ Fear of dying

__ Peer relationships

__ Possibility of a world war

__ Knowing God

Most of today's parents remember the day John F. Kennedy was shot. We probably remember where we were. Who told us. Maybe even what we were wearing or doing at the time. And most of us probably cried. But to help you see the contrast between generations, consider the reaction of one twentysomething "buster" to a more recent national tragedy:

> I was in…class when the space shuttle Challenger blew up. Some of the teachers actually started to cry, but what did we do? By the next day, most of my friends were trading our favorite "Christa McAuliffe's Spring Break" jokes by the Coke machine. This syndrome has manifested itself everywhere from our reaction to the Berlin Wall coming down ("I guess that means [they'll] get Happy Meals now") to my own flippant response—"Oh, really?"—when I was told on the phone that my parents were getting divorced.
>
> The hardest thing about being young right now is being…unable to let ourselves believe in anything.[7]

Answers: Life goals (1), school (2), knowing God (3), peers (4), career (5), war (6), family (7), dying (8). Source: *Today's Teens: A Generation in Transition*, © 1991 Barna Research Group, p. 16.

As a Christian teen, you may read this and think, *What's this guy's problem? I don't have those kinds of attitudes. Let him speak for himself.*

Okay, so maybe *you* don't share his cynicism. But many of your peers do. And as you read the following statistics about your generation, ask yourself whether these describe you.

■ 57% say they are skeptics (have trouble trusting or believing in people).

■ Two out of five say they are "stressed out." (This figure is nearly double that of older adults). In fact, 47% think they're "too busy."

Think about 1 Peter 1:24-25. Man's opinions come and go, but whose standards are timeless?

■ 35% feel it is "nearly impossible to have a successful family anymore." One in four don't think of marriage as "permanent." 60% think it would be best to live together before marriage and 50% think cohabiting will actually *replace* marriage.

■ Yet 71% of these same young people still believe that "families would be happier if the mother…stays home with the children."

■ A whopping 98% believe that parents should have "a lot" of influence on the values of their kids. But only 21% said that parents actually do. Peers (39%) and the media (24%) won out over parents.

■ Only 19% say that schools should teach abstinence before marriage. The vast majority (69%) feel that teaching about birth control should be the "preferred position" of schools.[8]

And what about their relationship with God? Nine out of ten say they believe in God or a "higher power," while one in four claim to be "born again." Yet we can see by the other statistics (and some important ones you'll find in Study Six) that beliefs and claims aren't making a significant difference in the lives of today's young people. Searching for truth that goes beyond Sunday morning talk, they are hungry. Hungry for more than religion and a lifeless list of dos and don'ts. Twenty-year-old Lisa puts it this way:

> ❝ Teenagers…need a clearly defined value system against which to test other values and discover their own. But when the important adults in their lives don't know what their own values are and are not sure what is right and what is wrong, what is good and what is bad, the teenagers' task is even more difficult.[9] ❞
>
> **—David Elkind**

I grew up in a very religious home. [But] all I want is reality. Show me God. Tell me what he is really

like....I don't want the empty promises. I want the
real thing. And I'll go wherever I find that truth
system.[10]

Digging deeper: What
does God promise to
those who are hungry?
(Read Matthew 5:6)

These are today's youths. They want more than words.
They want to *see* that Christianity really works. Deep
inside they seem to know what's right. Yet they don't have
the training or the courage to live it. Most have never
seen authentic Christianity on display. Sadly, they've
never known an uncompromising Christian!

If you're satisfied with living and looking and thinking
just like the world around you, you're probably not going
to enjoy this book. But the fact that you've read even this
far suggests that you're different—that you want to throw
off the mistrusting, sarcastic, compromising attitudes of
your peers and live God's way. As you make your way
through these pages, we'll offer suggestions on how you
can be trained (or "discipled" as the Bible would say) to
stand up courageously for what you believe—and *show*
your peers that God is real!

---

3 What is there about you that would convince others
who are your age that Christianity really works?

It's Time To Question *Conformity*!

We're not too old to remember wanting to be different
from our parents. One set of parents listened to country
music, the other to "Big Band" and "Top 40." We were
turned off by both. As soon as we got into the car, we
twisted the radio dial to good old WPGC to find the
Rolling Stones, Rod Stewart or The Who. Then, without
even checking the volume, we'd automatically turn it up.

Our parents are from the south. Our moms liked to cook lots of weird-tasting, fried vegetables. We liked pizza and burgers. (Not that we ever actually *tasted* the vegetables, but we could tell by looking at them we didn't like them.)

And our parents liked Sunday mornings at the church. Organs. Suits and dresses. Hymns. Stained glass windows. Eloquent teachings from the Old Testament. Choir members in robes with off-white tassels around their necks. Polite smiles to friends while slipping quietly into beautiful wooden pews.

That was a little stuffy for us, but we loved our Thursday night youth meetings. Sitting on the basement floor in the church building. Bell-bottomed jeans and bare feet. Guitars and tambourines. Simple songs written by new converts just off drugs (you can imagine what some of them sounded like!). Yells across the room to greet a new arrival. Unrehearsed thoughts about a favorite Bible passage.

Every generation feels the strong desire to be different. Some of this is rooted in pride: wanting to distance yourself from—or even rebel against—those in authority (we called them "the establishment" in the '60s). But a part of this longing is an inner desire to grow. To express yourself in the unique way God made you. To discover the ways your generation can *do* something, as generations before have. To be known and respected for achieving some kind of success.

Think about Hebrews 13:17. Though written about church leaders, this passage perfectly describes how teens should respond to their parents' authority.

It's not hard for us to remember how strongly we felt about things when we were teens. But we have to confess. Something happened in the last twenty years and suddenly we've become "the establishment." The grown-ups. The people the guy was thinking about when he created the bumper sticker that says, "QUESTION AUTHORITY."

It happened to our parents and now it's happening to us. We can't understand why teens in the mall wear jeans big enough for three and boots that must weigh 100 pounds. We occasionally watch snatches of MTV, realizing much of what teens today watch would have been rated X when we were their age. And from the little we've heard on the radio, we understand why some of the popular tunes are called "alternative music"—they're unlike anything we've ever heard before.

So we shake our heads and mumble the way our moms and dads did, "What's happening to this generation?"

Some of our reactions come simply because we're parents—and parents are not supposed to like the hairstyles, clothes, or music of the upcoming generation. If we did, teen culture would have to find even stranger ways to prove it was different. (Don't tell anybody, but we actually *do* like some of the current styles!) And yet the basis of our concern is much deeper. We carry a burden for today's young people that goes beyond how you dress or what music you like.

> ❝ Too old to be children, too young to enter the adult world, with bodies and minds capable of adult activities (such as having children), passionately desiring to be taken seriously, they hang between two worlds: not really children and not really adults, and yet somehow both at the same time.[11] ❞
>
> —**Michael Keating**

As we already mentioned, teens, you are part of what's been called the "lost generation." Millions of your peers have been lost to abortion since the 1973 Supreme Court decision that legalized abortion on demand. Thousands are lost each year to drug overdoses, alcohol-related traffic deaths, suicide, crime, and—at a rapidly increasing rate—to AIDS.

Others have held onto their lives, but they've lost hope that marriage and family life can be successful. They've lost faith in an all-powerful God who sees and knows and loves them. And they've lost the courage to say "no" to compromise and sin.

The "lost generation" isn't limited to the directionless teens you see hanging around on street corners during the evening news. Many of today's churched youth, whose parents tried to raise them to know and serve God, have been lost to worldliness. And many parents don't even know it.

Jesus had a special concern for lost things. Listen to what he said:

> Suppose one of you has a hundred sheep and loses one of them. Does he not leave the ninety-nine in the open country and go after the lost sheep until he finds it?...Or suppose a woman has ten silver coins and loses one. Does she not light a lamp, sweep the house and search carefully until she finds it? (Luke 15:4,8)
>
> For the Son of Man came to seek and to save what was lost (Luke 19:10).

Digging deeper: What does 2 Peter 3:9 tell you about God's feelings toward the lost?

God's heart for the lost is clear. If a sheep or a coin is worth such a careful search, then certainly an entire generation of precious young people are. We believe God is on a search for this "lost generation." You aren't invisible to him! His search is not to find you but to *use* those of you who will abandon yourselves to him.

Young men, will you be part of the army of radical, counter-culture teens God is raising up to become *visible* in your generation? Not visible because of how you dress or how many pounds you can bench-press. But visible because you dare to be different for the cause of Christ and the advance of his kingdom in your generation?

Young women, are you willing to explode the myth that being a teenager means being self-centered? Argumentative? Rebellious to authority? Looking for ways to bend the rules? Easily tempted? Absorbed with making yourself attractive to guys?

---

4 Some teens dream of becoming a pro quarterback... an actor or actress...an inner-city evangelist. What dreams do *you* have for the future? (Briefly write them below.) Ask God to show you *his* exciting plans for you!

Before every act of creation, we once heard, there's an act of destruction. That's definitely true here. Before God can create in you the courage and radical ability to take your stand for what's right and fulfill his call on your life, some destruction will take place. God must first destroy your pride. Your selfishness. Your "things have to go my way" attitude. Your resistance to your parents' authority. Your craving for acceptance and popularity.

> **The most solid preventive action we can take to protect and preserve the next generation is to help them develop a biblical worldview when they are children.**[12]
>
> —Fran Sciacca

Jesus said, "Whoever finds his life will lose it, and whoever loses his life for my sake will find it" (Matthew 10:39). Those teens who choose to lose their lives for Christ—who surrender themselves totally to him—will have an explosive impact on their generation.

Parents, we've got a price to pay as well. Too many Christian parents today expect more *from* their teens than they have invested *in* them. Our generation has given itself to selfish pursuits, often at the expense of our children. What we do in moderation, they tend to do in excess. Are we prepared to be honest and admit where we have led by example…toward compromise? God doesn't reject us for our failures. But he holds us responsible for the legacy of worldliness we have left to our kids.

Think about 2 Corinthians 10:4-5.
When it came to removing things that opposed God's will, Paul was a demolitions expert!

We, too, have to explode the myth of what it means to parent teenagers. And we shouldn't be surprised to see a lot of debris. Unbiblical ways of thinking. A lack of courage to provide costly leadership. Sinful reactions and attitudes toward our children. But as these things are blown out of the way, we'll be free to train this generation of future warriors for Jesus Christ.

Are you ready to push the plunger? To demolish all the myths standing between you and God's wonderful plan for parents and teens? Then offer this as a heartfelt prayer to God…and let the fireworks begin.

Jesus, I commit myself to hearing what you're trying to say to me as I study this book. I humble myself today to allow your Holy Spirit to search my heart and life. Please help me to overcome anything that will prevent me from being the teenager/parent you've called me to be. I want our family life to bring glory to you! Help me to be honest with myself and my teen/parents, even when it's hard or awkward. Thank you for this time you've set aside for us to work on our relationship. In Jesus' name. Amen. ■

QUESTIONS FOR PARENTS 1. Which of the following movie titles best states your expectations of the teen years? (A) *Nightmare on Elm Street*, (B) *The Good, The Bad and The Ugly*, (C) *It's A Wonderful Life*

2. Based on the definitions given in this study (Page 3), does your child act more like a "youth" or a "teenager"?

3. Do you expect your child to rebel during adolescence? If possible, discuss your answer with someone whose counsel and biblical knowledge you respect.

4. How well do you understand the "baby buster" generation? Rate youself on a scale of 1 (clueless) to 10 (expert).

5. Do you demand more of your teen than you demand of yourself? In what areas?

QUESTIONS FOR TEENS

1. Complete the following sentence in your own words: "The main purpose of the teen years is to…"

2. How well do you think your parents understand your generation? Rate them from 1 (clueless) to 10 (expert).

3. If you had to speak on behalf of all teens, how would you answer this question: "What does your generation want most in life?"

4. Do you look forward to being an adult? Why or why not?

FACE TO FACE

1. Come up with three adjectives each describing what it's like when you spend time together. (Examples: "fun," "tense," "nonexistent")

2. How would you define the difference between rebellion and a legitimate desire to be different? (Think of specific examples.)

3. Take turns describing one person you admire, and why.

4. Discuss "Ten Myths About Teens And Parents" (Page 6). Do you agree with the authors? With each other?

RECOMMENDED READING

Fran Sciacca, *Generation At Risk* (Chicago, IL: Moody Press, 1991)

Answer to Warm-Up
(from page 1): Using these estimates, it would cost Albanian citizens $33,600,000 dollars to blow up all their bunkers. That's a costly myth!

IMAGE IS EVERYTHING

BIBLE STUDY   1 Samuel 16:1-13

WARM-UP   Teenagers are *big* spenders. The 20.5 million teens living in the United States spend around $93 *billion* each year! (That means the average teen spends $4,536.59 every 12 months...wow!) On which of the following items do you think teens spend most of their fortune?

❑ Gifts for friends/relatives   ❑ Books and magazines

❑ Records/tapes/CDs   ❑ Personal care products

❑ Clothes and accessories   ❑ Hobbies

(See page 33 for answer)

PERSONAL STUDY   He was the perfect spokesman in the commercial for Canon's "Rebel" camera. Great physique. Trendy haircut. Earring. Tons of talent. Confidence. And attitude.

He's Andre Agassi. And in one short phrase he caught the heartbeat of today's youth culture.

"Image is everything!"

We certainly got wrapped up in the "image" thing as teens. I (Benny) was kind of a mixed bag. Because I played football, I had some friends in the "jock" crowd. But I mostly hung around with the "greasers" (known for the grease they put in their hair) and "heads" (short for "pot-heads"). They were the ones who partied a lot. Went to the "Rod and Custom" car shows every year. Experimented with drugs. Wore tie-dyed jeans and had long hair. Didn't get too excited about studies or school activities.

Sheree, though, was very "collegiate." She enjoyed studying and being involved in school clubs and activities. Her crowd was clean-cut and athletic. They partied only for a "reason"—to celebrate the basketball team's victory or opening night of the spring musical. The guys wore short hair and the girls shopped at the newest, most trendy stores. And they never associated with my friends.

(We're glad God brought us together—that's a story of its own!)

The terms "greasers" and "heads" may be antiques by now, but the attitudes haven't changed. Teens still label themselves and each other. You find the group with the label you like. Then you dress, act, and talk like the people in the group to be accepted by them. Unless you're a "poser." Then you adjust according to the group you happen to be with that day.

It's all about image.

Most people care about their image, but none focus on it more intensely than teens. During these critical years, they are forming opinions of themselves—"mental pictures" based largely on feedback they get from others.

As teens, you naturally want to be accepted. Liked. Sought after for friendship (especially by the kids who are popular). The image you project will have a big impact on your popularity and influence. So you certainly don't want to project the "wrong" image. That's why you're very careful about choosing the group you want to be in. And then you have to make sure everybody knows it by how you dress, who you hang around with, and what your interests are.

Digging deeper: Can you find the Bible's term for being overly concerned with the opinions of others? (See Proverbs 29:25) Why is this called a "snare"?

> ❝ Take a quick glance into any adolescent girl's bedroom, and what do you usually find—ad pages torn out of fashion and life-style magazines such as *Teen*, *Glamour*, *Cosmopolitan*, *Elle*, or *Vogue*. Why do they do this? Is something wrong with their parents' choice of wallpaper? The ads provide teen eyes with a map of what's hot and what's not. Actually, these images are more than a map. They represent the standard by which an impressionable teen will measure herself.[1] ❞
>
> —**Robert G. DeMoss, Jr.**

Or maybe you're one of those who refuse to play such juvenile games. You purposefully dress to please nobody but you. You think it's foolish to conform to what everybody else is wearing or saying or doing. You take pride in being different than everyone else. (Except for all the other "individualists" who dress and act like you as you isolate yourself from all the "conformists"!)

We don't mean to be sarcastic. The point is this: We're all concerned about our image. Let's admit it. The clone who acts and dresses exactly like her friends is no different than the guy who thinks he's refusing to conform—and laughs with his buddies at those who are. Both have a reputation at stake.

1 See if you can match the terms on the left with their definitions on the right. (Answers are printed upside down at bottom of page…you'll need 'em, parents!)

1. Skaters	A. Nerds, geeks, dorks
2. Headbangers	B. Rednecks, stompers, hicks, country/western music lovers
3. Posers	C. Rappers
4. Preppies	D. Thrashers; skateboarders who wear pants big enough for the whole family
5. Bassers	E. Phonies who "wanna be" like a certain group but aren't; projecting an image
6. Kickers	F. Bashers; followers of heavy metal music
7. Dweebs	G. Collegiates

Do You Know What You're Known For?

Janet is just embarking on adolescence. At 13, she's becoming more and more concerned about how she's viewed by others. If there's an upcoming birthday party—especially for one of the popular kids in her "group"—she's eager to know if she's been invited. She calls around to see what the other girls are wearing to make sure she won't be over- or under-dressed for an event. She often asks her friends if they like her new outfit or haircut. And she's very curious about what the guys think of her. ("Do you think he thinks I'm pretty? Would you ask him?")

At 16, Derrick's reputation is well-developed. He's known for his big appetite (so he always eats a lot, even when he's not hungry). His athletic skills (so he played basketball last season even though his grades were already suffering from football season). And his popularity among the best-looking girls (so he flirts with them even though his parents have warned where that can lead).

Like many teens, Janet and Derrick have fallen into the "image is everything" trap. By projecting a certain image, they are gaining a reputation in specific areas. Now they must strive to live up to this reputation.

Digging deeper: Read Proverbs 2:12-15. When does popularity become dangerous?

(Answers: 1-D, 2-F, 3-E, 4-G, 5-C, 6-B, 7-A)

17

How can a teen tell when he or she has become too concerned about reputation? Here are three giveaways:

Preoccupation with appearance. You identify with a certain image and seek to reflect it with your clothing, make-up, jewelry and hairstyle. Even small details like the size of your earrings or the brand-name of your tennis shoes take on incredible significance.

Concern for popularity. You begin bending your Christian values in order to gain friends, and consider it more important to spend time with them than with your family and church.

Focus on abilities rather than character. You find yourself working hard in those areas where you get attention and approval—athletics, music, drama, scholastics, and so on. As wholesome and "good" as these may be, they can easily become the source of your identity and divert your heart from the more critical issues of character.

Even the prophet Samuel—one of the most discerning men in Israel's history—temporarily fell into the "image is everything" mode. God had sent him to Bethlehem to anoint a king from among the sons of Jesse. One of the sons, Eliab, immediately caught Samuel's attention. He was tall and handsome—good king material, assumed Samuel. And yet God quickly clarified that Eliab was not the man for the job: "Do not consider his *appearance* or his height, for I have rejected him. The Lord does not look at the things man looks at. *Man looks at the outward appearance, but the Lord looks at the heart*" (1 Samuel 16:7, emphasis added).

Samuel checked out seven of Jesse's other sons, but none met God's requirements. Finally Jesse called his youngest son, David, from the fields. And as you know, this was God's man.

Did God reject Eliab *because* he was tall and handsome? Obviously not, because David himself had "a fine appearance and handsome features" (vs. 12). But God saw something in David he didn't see in his older brother.

David had more than looks. He had character.

CHARACTER IS...

■ How you act when your parents say you can't use the car.

■ What you do when your sister doesn't return your Walkman.

■ How you respond when your face breaks out the morning of school pictures.

■ The reason you give for being in a bad mood.

■ How you react when your mom corrects you for not cleaning your room.

■ What you feel inside when your best friend gets a higher grade on the exam.

Are You Playing Favorites?

Why isn't character as important to us as it is to God? And why do teens pay such special attention to how they—and others—look and dress? The Bible gives us a clear answer:

> My brothers, as believers in our glorious Lord Jesus Christ, don't show favoritism. Suppose a man comes into your meeting wearing a gold ring and fine clothes, and a poor man in shabby clothes also comes in. If you show special attention to the man wearing fine clothes and say, "Here's a good seat for you," but say to the poor man, "You stand there" or "Sit on the floor by my feet," have you not discriminated among yourselves and become judges with evil thoughts?…But if you show favoritism, you sin and are convicted by the law as lawbreakers (James 2:1-4, 9).

What God is saying is this: Don't deceive yourself. You don't just focus on outward things because you prefer a certain "look," are attracted to a particular personality type, or like people who are tall. Dark. Slim. Blonde. Smart. Athletic. Funny. Wealthy. Outgoing. Or whatever.

When you pick friends because of how they look or act, you are showing favoritism: discriminating, judging, and being motivated by sinful attitudes rather than love.

Sound serious? It *is*—or the Bible wouldn't be so strong on this issue.

The passage from James may seem a little outdated, so we've taken the liberty to rephrase it in the language of today's teen:

Digging deeper: Read Acts 10 (especially vs. 34-35). How was Peter showing favoritism? How did God adjust him?

> As Christian young people, stop giving others special treatment based on what they look like. Say a visitor comes into the youth meeting wearing cool clothes and $120 tennis shoes. Right behind him comes a guy wearing a geeky outfit and last year's shoes off the K-Mart sale rack. If you greet the first guy and invite him to sit with you, but ignore the other guy and leave him to sit alone, you've got a problem. And it's a big one.

How can you know if you're guilty of favoritism? Here are some questions to ask yourself.

■ Do you check out what people look like or how they are dressed before you reach out to them?

■ Are you motivated to get to know someone based on his athletic ability? Her popularity? Size? Clothes?

■ Would others easily identify you as being in a certain "clique" in your school or youth group?

■ Do you and your friends all dress, wear your hair, and act like each other?

■ Do you usually look for and hang out with your "group" members in school or church meetings?

■ If asked, would the less popular (by your definition) kids in your school or youth group describe you as too "cool" for them? Unfriendly? Busy with other friendships?

■ Do you envy others for the way they look, the things they own, or the attention they get?

■ Do you avoid certain people because you're embarrassed to be seen with them? Do you purposely pursue those you're proud to be seen with?

> 66 The media parade impossible examples...before the young and make it seem as if those who do not have these qualities are simply not worth much. The result? An incredibly large number of young people, even many of those who actually *are* talented, popular, and attractive by youth standards, have enormous self-image problems.[2] 99
> —Michael Keating

If you've answered "Yes" to any of these, you probably have a problem with favoritism. You can be pretty sure some people around you have noticed it...and, perhaps, been hurt by it.

Why not stop now and confess this sin to God? Ask for his forgiveness and help to change. What impresses him is *character*. Start looking beyond what others look like and you'll find yourself impressed by what God sees in them!

Help For A "Hurting Unit"

While Benny hung out with the "heads," I (Sheree) was, in many ways, a model teenager. I studied hard and stayed away from the rowdy kids in school. I sang in the school choir and even worked in the principal's office. I was also very involved in my church.

Those who knew me would have described me as confident. Together. Wholesome. Always smiling cheerfully, and hanging out with the jocks and cheerleaders.

But much of what others saw was pure "image." Behind the scenes I was hurting. My older brother had recently been paralyzed in a swimming accident and was critically ill. My sister was going through a divorce. Financial struggles in the family had just forced us to move to a smaller home in a rough neighborhood, and my younger brother was getting involved with the wrong crowd. At the time I was dating a guy who was not a Christian, and it was having a bad effect on my relationship with God. With Dad working lots of overtime and Mom spending long days at the hospital, I was carrying a lot more responsibility in the home as well as watching out for my little brother. That left me with less time for my studies, so my grades had started to slip.

And none of my friends knew any of this was happening.

Behind the smiles and the confidence, I was what a friend of ours would call "a hurting unit." But my image was too important to me. I couldn't let anyone know how lonely and sad I really was.

Think about Proverbs 17:17. How does a *true* friend treat you when you don't have it all together?

---

2 If a newspaper reporter asked your friends to describe you, what kinds of words would they use? (Examples: "Tough," "funny," "cool")

Would they be describing the *real* you or just your image?

Had I been diagnosed today, a counselor probably would have said I was struggling with "low self-esteem." Finances rarely allowed for the "right" clothes. My responsibilities at home caused me to feel left out of the fun things my friends were doing. I didn't want to have people over much because our apartment was small. Overnighters with girlfriends didn't work because I shared a room with my 10-year-old brother. And the old, mostly red Falcon I drove—with various colors of primer covering its rust and dents—was in serious need of a new exhaust system (and everybody knew it!).

No, from a worldly point of view, there wasn't a whole lot to make a 16-year-old girl feel good about herself. So it became critical for me to protect my image, to hide the "me" inside. I was afraid of all that was happening in my family. Resentful of my duties at home. Embarrassed about the car I drove and the neighborhood where we lived. Too proud to open up and let others see what was really happening. And feeling sorry for myself for it all.

Life was hard.

Had someone given me tips for beefing up my self-esteem, it might have made me feel better. All of us want to feel important and know we're valued. To have been told I was significant and special would have felt great. (Though you should know that despite everything happening in their lives, I always felt my parents' deep love. Thank you, Mom and Dad!)

But merely *feeling* better about myself wouldn't have changed any of my circumstances. In fact, giving me a pep talk on self-esteem would have been the worst thing anyone could have done to me.

Why? Because my self-esteem levels were already dangerously high!

Be forewarned: What we're about to say is controversial. And yet it's entirely biblical. For Scripture's teaching on self collides head-on with what is popular. Today's books, articles, and talk shows assume that teens are desperately short on self-esteem, and need massive injections of it in order to survive adolescence. Yet from our experience, the teens who esteem themselves least and esteem *others* most have—by far—the healthiest self-image.

How Much Are You Worth?

We discover a great deal about our worth in the Bible. We have been "fearfully and wonderfully made" (Psalm 139:14). We have the prospect of an exciting and fulfilling future (Jeremiah 29:11). We can be used by the Holy Spirit to perform miracles and preach the gospel (Luke 4:18-19). Because of the death and resurrection of Jesus Christ we are of *great* value to God. He loves us and has a unique plan for our lives.

This is all wonderfully true. But why? Is it because, like the L'Oreal hair commercial says, we're "worth it"?

Hardly. There's only one reason why God loves us. Only one reason why we can be used by the Holy Spirit and have hope for the future. Only one reason why we have any value at all in God's sight.

King David gives us an important insight: "Surely I have been a sinner from birth, sinful from the time my

Digging deeper: What characteristics does God esteem in a person? (See Isaiah 66:2)

mother conceived me" (Psalm 51:5). Many other passages echo this theme, stressing over and over that there is *nothing* in you or anyone worthy of God's love and acceptance. Even our very best deeds are like "filthy rags" in light of his holiness (Isaiah 64:6).

And yet, by the totally undeserved grace of a merciful God, we have been made the apple of his eye. His precious possession. His chosen treasure.

> **❝** How long is it going to take God to free us from the morbid habit of thinking about ourselves? We must get sick unto death of ourselves, until there is no longer any surprise at anything God can tell us about ourselves. We cannot touch the depths of meanness in ourselves. There is only one place where we are right, and that is in Christ Jesus.[3] **❞**
>
> —**Oswald Chambers**

Our point is this: What many call "self-esteem" is nothing more than self-love. The Bible never encourages you to find worth in who *you* are. In fact, it warns us of how wicked we are (Jeremiah 17:9). For the best any of us had to offer sent Jesus Christ to the cross.

Parents and teens, our worth is found only in the fact that God redeemed us by his grace and is remaking us in his image. And in order for him to make us in his image, we must resist the infectious disease of self-love that plagues today's culture.

Self-love isn't a teenage developmental problem. It's a sin problem. It plagues young and old, male and female, in every nation on earth. And many sincere but misguided Christians are making the problem worse by the way they interpret this part of the Bible:

Think about 2 Timothy 3:2. Is self-love seen here as a positive thing or a negative thing?

'Love the Lord your God with all your heart and with all your soul and with all your mind.' This is the first and greatest commandment. And the second is like it: 'Love your neighbor as yourself' (Matthew 22:37-39).

By saying "Love your neighbor as yourself," they argue, Jesus was suggesting we must all learn to love ourselves in order to best love those around us.

We disagree. So do most Christian scholars.

When you look at one passage by itself, it can mean almost anything. But when you read Jesus' remark in light of other related passages in the Bible, it is obvious that he was coming from a very different angle. Knowing that the human heart is self-centered and sinful by nature, Jesus was making an important assumption in this passage.

Let's look at it again: "Love your neighbor *as* [meaning *as much as*] you love yourself." In other words, Jesus was saying we'll please God by learning to love others as much as we *already* love ourselves. And that's a lot of love.

---

3 You get a flyer in the mail advertising a weekend seminar titled, "Learn To Love Yourself!" For the low, low price of $99, you'll learn all the following valuable tips. (Check the ones you don't already know, then decide: Is it worth the price?)

❏ How to get the last piece of pie…every time

❏ How to sulk when friends leave you out

❏ How to obtain your own credit card

❏ How to blame teammates for *your* mistakes

❏ How to keep your body from waking up early

❏ How to spend $100 on nobody but you

Dead Men Don't Wear Levis

The teen years are a challenging time. Physical and emotional changes are taking place. New temptations and desires are surfacing. Pressures about school, holding down a part-time job, or choosing a college can be intense. The desire to be treated like a responsible adult clashes with the urge to act like the carefree child you were just a few short years ago.

Your parents expect more of you and depend more on you. Sometimes it seems your math teacher assigns work as if hers is the only class you're taking. Then there are the piano lessons. Work. Money for car insurance or new football cleats. Oh, no—braces! Chores around the house. Youth meetings. School clubs. Tension between you and a friend. An English exam. Acne.

You couldn't wait to become a teenager. If only you had realized how overwhelming it would be at times.

What you are experiencing are growing pains. It's not easy learning to think and act responsibly, to get serious about things that meant little to you only a few years ago (such as school, finances, and preparing for your future). It's not easy to have self-control when you feel like yelling at your little brother. Learning to manage your life with all its new pressures can be frustrating and stressful. But it's all part of growing up.

Being absorbed with yourself won't help you mature any faster. Self-love will only slow you down, making you resist and complain about the important things God is seeking to do in your life.

If anyone had a right to moan about his circumstances, it was Paul. It seemed like he was always being thrown in jail, beaten, robbed, shipwrecked, bitten by snakes, and abandoned by friends. His life could have been one long pity party. Instead, here was his attitude:

> I have been crucified with Christ and I no longer live, but Christ lives in me. The life I live in the body, I live by faith in the Son of God, who loved me and gave himself for me (Galatians 2:20).

Teens, here lies the only solid foundation for your identity. If you are a Christian, you are *dead* to yourself. And "dead" men and women aren't driven by selfish desires. They have no need to impress others. To be liked and accepted. To make the grades or get the dates.

Your worth is found in Jesus Christ alone. He is your life. No award or relationship or popularity contest in this world can bring you a sense of value like he can. You will best find your worth when you realize that without him, you're worth*less*. And this is just the realization that began turning things around for that 16-year-old girl named Sheree.

Self-love will always be accepted and encouraged by our godless society. Everything around you says, "Promote yourself. Strive for recognition. Assert your independence. Get ahead, even if you have to walk over others. Indulge yourself. Blame others for your mistakes and failures. Draw attention to yourself. Use others to your advantage. Be young. Have fun. Live for the moment."

Digging deeper: Read 1 Corinthians 1:26-31. Did Paul find it necessary to "stroke" the Corinthians' self-esteem?

❝ Young minds are like sponges. They need to be careful about what puddle they are sitting in.[4] ❞
—Dr. Robert Laurent

And young people are buying it. Teens kill their peers for a pair of tennis shoes. They criticize and spread lies about a former friend for "stealing" a boyfriend. They invest incredible amounts of money on make-up and clothing and expensive hair products to get the right "look." And without even realizing it, they are wasting some of the most precious years of their lives in a prison of self-love.

We "me generation" parents—including most of those in the church—have raised primped, pampered, polished teens who think self-love is normal. And most people call this "healthy."

Are you looking for love? Acceptance? Worth? Security? Do you want to feel significant even though you admit you're just a normal teen with average looks and talents?

Then follow in the footsteps of Jesus, who "came not to be served, but to serve" (Matthew 20:28). No one in history ever had a healthier self-image than he did. But you'll have to walk the same road he did. Deny yourself. Look for ways to promote and honor others. Rely not on yourself but on God. Take responsibility for your failures. Respect and submit to authority. Maximize your teen years in service to others. Give this critical time in your life to God.

If you've submitted your life to Jesus Christ, he accepts you as his child. He loves you unconditionally. But every loving parent has expectations of a child, and God is no different. He wants to help you grow. And he wants to help you overcome self-love so you can experience the adventure of seeing your life really count in the kingdom of God.

---

4 Consider the following statement: *I no longer care what others think of me, as long as I please God.* In order for that statement to be true, would you have to make any changes in the areas of your life listed below?

❑ Use of time

❑ Use of money

❑ Friendships

❑ Activities

Ten Symptoms Of Self-Love

Are you in love with yourself? Most of us are. As we developed the following list, *we* were freshly convicted of some things in our lives.

Please be honest with yourself as you read these. But don't allow the enemy to crush you with condemnation. God doesn't expose the sin in our hearts to make us feel guilty. He convicts us so that we'll repent and allow him to change us.

Think about Hebrews 4:12. When God does surgery on us, he does it with the sharp scalpel of his Word...not with a baseball bat!

Remember, God is patient, merciful, and kind. When Satan accuses you of being unworthy, agree with him... but then point to the cross. For while you were still his enemy, God loved you so much that he sent Jesus to die for your sins. And the One who began this great work in you promises to bring it to completion (Philippians 1:6).

An overemphasis on your appearance. Clothes, make-up, hairstyle, accessories, or weight.

Self-pity about "flaws" you can't change. Size of your nose, ears, feet, or anything else; height; scars; facial features; hair texture or color; lack of athletic ability; race.

Tearing others down to build yourself up. Proudly comparing yourself to others; looking for things to criticize, especially in those you envy; speaking critically of someone to try and influence people to dislike him/her.

Self-importance. Dominating conversations with talk about yourself (how many points you scored, what you did over the weekend); taking advantage of others to get what you want; asking for money to buy things when you know it would be tough for your parents; assuming that nothing is more important or interesting than the details of *your* life.

> 💬 Youth exist in a kind of media-made ghetto, where views of the meaning of life, categories of success, and images of manhood and womanhood have little to do with reality...Many winners in the youth world end up losers as adults.[5]
>
> —**Michael Keating**

Moodiness. Frequently giving in to selfish attitudes about how hard your life is; often being in a bad mood (Hint: You probably don't notice it—trust the input of those around you); taking out your frustrations on others (especially your family); not having self-control over your emotions (such as anger, self-pity, and irritation).

Greedy/selfish attitudes and desires. Not being content with your home, clothes, and belongings; insisting on shopping at the "right" places for the "right" clothes; resenting your parents' financial limitations; complaining about what you don't have; overreacting when someone takes the last donut or wants to watch a different TV show.

Hypocrisy. Being a "poser" by acting one way around your parents and Christian friends and another way around non-Christian friends; "playing the part" to hide worldly attitudes and actions; lying to cover up compromise.

Cocky or bossy attitudes toward others. Always needing to be right; finding it hard to admit wrong or failure; bossing your siblings or friends; arguing (even when you're not sure what you're talking about and you know it!); getting frustrated when things don't go your way.

Think about Proverbs 18:2. The fool likes nothing better than hearing himself talk.

Independent attitudes and behavior. Deciding it's time to change things like bedtime, TV selections, length of phone conversations, or eating habits without discussing it with your parents; not coming home on time; neglecting household chores or homework because you decided it wasn't really necessary; having an "I'm old enough to make my own decisions" attitude.

Minimal relationship with God. Thinking of spiritual things as boring; doing things with Christians and the church mainly because that's what's expected, not because you want to; spending little time with God because too many "more important things" are going on; having a mechanical or non-existent devotional life.

Don't just glance over these areas. Take an honest look at yourself. Parents, discuss this list with your teen. We have also found it helpful to get feedback from someone outside our family. (Even though that can be a bit scary!)

You shouldn't be surprised if you occasionally stumble in some of these areas. But please don't explain away these symptoms. If, after close inspection, you determine they are happening regularly, then you definitely have a case of self-love. And you want to get rid of it as fast as possible rather than making excuses or blame-shifting.

Think about Micah 7:19. Once we've repented of our sins, where does God put them?

Again, there's no reason to despair or feel hopeless. Genuine conviction by the Holy Spirit always brings *hope* for change. When we confess our sin, he will both forgive *and* cleanse us. With God's help, you can become a different person—free from self-love and "eager to do what is good" (Titus 2:11-14).

Learning To Look At Internals

Craig became a Christian at age 12. He was physically mature beyond his years. Handsome. Well-built. Outgoing. But it was easy to see no one had taught him much about

28

humility. He talked a lot about the older girls who flirted with him, thinking he was their age. He frequently wore clothes that drew attention to his physique. He made sure he sat with the girls in class or on church outings. At youth meetings he could always be expected to answer the most questions, yet he spoke little about his relationship with the Lord around non-Christians.

> **Fool:** One who acts contrary to sound wisdom in his moral deportment; one who follows his own inclinations, who prefers trifling and temporary pleasures to the service of God.
>
> —*Webster's Dictionary* **(1828 version)**

Craig was pretty proud of who he was and what others thought about him.

That was several years ago. Today, Craig is a different young man. Now he's quick to distance himself from flirtatious girls, and much more modest with his clothes. His closest friends are guys. He still contributes to the youth meetings…when he has something worth saying. It's easy to see he enjoys worship, and he is very outspoken about his relationship with God.

So what happened to Craig? Did he just "grow out of the adolescent phase" he was in? No. If that were possible, there wouldn't be so many adults still in love with themselves. Rather, after hearing someone teach about the dangers of self-love, Craig began to see himself with God's eyes. He didn't submit to condemnation—that often leads to self-pity, which is just another symptom of the disease! Instead, he acknowledged the truth. Repented. And began to make a couple of major changes.

First, he got serious about deepening his relationship with the Lord. No more Sunday-morning-only Christianity. He started having consistent devotions and began to express his love for God in worship. Second, Craig built new friendships with those who could inspire and challenge him. Rather than surround himself with friends he could easily impress, Craig got to know guys who impressed *him* with their maturity and strong character.

Digging deeper: Have you ever felt like the men described in John 12:42-43?

5 In the space below, name one peer whose character you admire. What is it you respect about him or her?

Character is a word often spoken but rarely explained. We can understand it a little better by looking at those things that matter so much in the teen world: athletic abilities, appearance, and good grades. Externals count most to teens. Character is the opposite of these. It involves *internal* things: Humility. Honesty. Compassion. Courage.

One of the fastest ways out of the "image is everything" trap is to start focusing on internals rather than externals. When you focus on externals—your batting average, your jeans size, your prize-winning essay—it's easy to be impressed with yourself. Especially when your evaluation of yourself is pretty positive. It's harder to impress yourself (or others) when you evaluate yourself by inner character.

God will give you plenty of surprise opportunities to evaluate your character. He puts us in situations—often uncomfortable situations—that reveal what's deep inside us. It's been said that pressure introduces you to yourself. Pressures don't *create* sinful attitudes or actions; they simply *expose* them. It's in those tense, unplanned moments that you see yourself for who you really are.

Turn Up The Heat!

A strong man bends over the huge vat of gold melting over the fire. He stirs the hot mixture and inserts a thermometer. Is it still at the right temperature? No. It's cooling down some. So he adds more wood to the fire. The heat causes the impurities in the gold to rise to the surface. Without enough heat the gold will never become pure.

Soon bubbles rise to the surface. The goldsmith reaches for the ladle. Slowly but expertly he skims the oily impurities—called dross—from the top of the vat.

He stirs some more. Adds more wood. Removes more dross. Over and over he repeats the process. Only when he can clearly see his reflection in the gold does he know he's finished. The refining process is complete, and the gold is fit for its purpose.

Digging deeper: Read Malachi 3:2-4. Have you ever thought of God as a bar of soap?!

God refines our character in much the same way. We are the gold. He brings the dross (sin) to the surface by "turning up the heat" in our lives. He knows he's finished when he sees his reflection—his character, attitudes, motives, and responses—in us.

If you can look at life's pressures this way it will change your whole attitude toward the teenage years. Don't resent God or others for the hassles. The inconveniences. The siblings who mess up your stuff. The guy who outscored you in the game. The authority of your parents. The way you look or the car you'll never have. Instead, see all these as part of your loving Father's plan to reveal the dross in your heart and get rid of it.

A lot of people have talent, looks, or appealing personalities. Like King David's big brother, Eliab. Fewer have character. Why? Because character development starts by kissing self-love goodbye. It also requires hard work, the gutsy perseverance Paul was describing when he said, "Be *diligent* in these matters; *give yourself wholly* to them, so that everyone may see your progress" (1 Timothy 4:15, emphasis added).

This process is what the Bible calls sanctification. (We'll talk about this more in Study Eight.) It begins at salvation, when God pardons your sin and declares you a new creation in Christ. But that's only the beginning. For as long as you live God will be shaping you into the image of Jesus. And Jesus was a man of exemplary character.

> 〝 It is good for us to encounter troubles and adversities from time to time, for trouble often compels a man to search his own heart. It reminds him that he is an exile here, and that he can put his trust in nothing in this world. It is good, too, that we sometimes suffer opposition, and that men think ill of us and misjudge us, even when we do and mean well. Such things are an aid to humility, and preserve us from pride and vainglory. For we more readily turn to God as our inward witness, when men despise us and think no good of us.[6] 〞
>
> —**Thomas a Kempis**

31

If you've been genuinely converted, thank God for delivering you from the penalty of your sin. But don't stop there. Cooperate with the Holy Spirit as he "raises the temperature" in your life to skim off those impurities of the heart that remain.

Think about Colossians 1:29. Sanctification is a struggle, but God gives us "all his energy" to insure we make it!

God doesn't expect you to become pure gold on your own. That's why he's given you role models in the church and parents to disciple you. Best of all, he has placed at your disposal the unlimited power of the Holy Spirit.

In closing, let's look again at the words of Andre Agassi. Is image really everything? No. At least not in the external way our culture emphasizes. And it's pitiful to see so many insecure teens pouring time and money and energy into themselves, chasing fantasies that will never come true.

But Andre was close. And a growing number of teens are realizing it. Having seen "self-esteem" for what it is, they've fallen out of love with themselves and in love with God. They are enthusiastic. Confident. At peace. Radical in their pursuit of Christ. And all for one reason.

Because *his* image in them *is* everything! ∎

QUESTIONS FOR PARENTS

1. Do you ever find yourself overly concerned about the opinion *your* peers have of you?

2. Which do you notice (and praise) more, your teen's character growth or external accomplishments?

3. Why, according to the authors, is "self-esteem" harmful to teens? (Page 23)

4. How would you describe the difference between self-love and a biblical self-image?

5. Does your teen see you responding joyfully when God "turns up the heat" in your life?

QUESTIONS FOR TEENS

1. Which of the following do your friends talk about a lot? (A) God, (B) clothes, (C) church activities, (D) music, (E) other friends, (F) school, (G) sports, (H) other.

2. What do your friends admire about you?

3. What does God admire about you?

4. "You will best find your worth when you realize that without [Jesus], you're worth*less*," say the authors (Page 25). Do you see their point?

5. What are some of the pressures and "growing pains" God is using in your life now to make you pure gold?

FACE TO FACE 1. Is it possible that disliking yourself (your straight hair, lack of coordination, etc.) could be self-love in disguise?

2. Why does God hate favoritism?

3. Review the "Ten Symptoms of Self-Love" and then talk about what "medication" could help cure the sickness.

4. Of the "Ten Character Traits For Teens" listed on page 30, which do you reflect? Which need some work?

5. What's the secret to not worrying about what others think of you?

6. How does the Holy Spirit help us reflect Christ's image?

RECOMMENDED READING Bill Hybels, *Descending Into Greatness* (Grand Rapids, MI: Zondervan Publishing, 1993)

Answer to Warm-Up
(from page 15): U.S. teens spend the most on clothes and accessories. One survey found 37.2% spend more than $50 per month on these items! Why? As the researchers concluded, "These products have image connotations." (Sources: Dennis Tootelian and Ralph Gaedeke, "The Teen Market," *The Journal of Consumer Marketing*, Fall '92; Peter Walsh, "Teen Spending: It's A Lot To Digest," *Daily News Record*, 9/6/93.)

STUDY THREE

PARENTS, TAKE YOUR PLACE!

BIBLE STUDY   Proverbs 22:6

WARM-UP   On a warm August night in 1984, gymnast Mary Lou Retton stood 73.5 feet away from the vaulting horse… and a gold medal. To win the all-round competition, she needed a perfect 10 in this final event. And she got it.

She had spent nine years getting ready for that single moment. But in her words, the pivotal point of her training came 18 months before when she made "that big leap." What was it?

(See page 50 for answer)

PERSONAL STUDY   We live in the suburbs of Washington, D.C., where teens are in serious crisis. They are killing their peers over clothes, portable CD players, drugs, or girlfriends. Last year alone, nearly 1,500 youths were arrested for crimes ranging from stealing cars to murder. Students attend schools with metal detectors and police patrols.

In January of 1994 several hundred D.C. teens met with their mayor to offer answers to the critical problems they are facing. Can you guess what their suggestions were?

- More money spent on education
- "Anger Management" seminars for students
- Government-funded job training so kids can work—instead of kill—for what they want
- Classes on the proper use of firearms
- More recreational facilities for after-school activities

You'll be surprised to hear that none of these suggestions were on the kids' minds. Unlike the bureaucrats who come up with the "solutions," these teens are the ones who hear the gunshots and risk being victimized by their peers every day. The only things they asked for were: "schools where they won't get shot, teachers they can talk to and classrooms where they can openly pray."[1]

These wise teens are on to some *real* solutions. We adults try to complicate everything. We foolishly assume that writing a check will always solve the problem. But money won't buy what these teens are looking for. They're simply looking for love, guidance, and help from adults...and they're looking for God.

Sadly, the most effective solution wasn't even mentioned: parental leadership and involvement. Why? Probably because our generation of parents has such a high "dropout" rate. Today's parents have selfishly and irresponsibly backed off and dropped out of their teens' lives. Consequently, a lost generation of lonely teens feels no one really cares anymore.

Dr. David Elkind, Professor of Child Study at Tufts University, describes the consequences of this lack of parental leadership and guidance in teens' lives:

> Because we are reluctant to take a firm stand, we deny teenagers the benefit of our parental concern and we impel them into premature adulthood. We say, "I don't know," but teenagers hear, "They don't care."[2]

So many of today's teens are growing up without parental training, guidance, and care. In some cases, parents are truly intimidated. "I *don't* know what to do with my teen," they say. "I don't really even know him or her anymore!" Unfortunately, few ever admit this to their children. Thinking that lack of involvement indicates a lack of love, these teens often try to shock their parents into action through sinful behavior. To escape the pressures of "premature adulthood" they turn to drugs. Alcohol. Acceptance and popularity among peers. Possessions and influence. Immorality. Power.

It's easy to see how this pattern could unfold in non-Christian homes of inner-city America. But all too many churchgoing families in neighborhoods throughout this nation have become battlegrounds for renegade parents and rebellious teens.

In your family, guns and drugs may not be problems. But the marks of parental irresponsibility and adolescent rebellion are often much more subtle. Like anger. Icy stares and stiff hugs. Heated arguments. Disrespectful attitudes. Moral compromise. Spiritual apathy. Bitterness.

And like many families, you're probably tempted to look the other way in hopes that "this, too, shall pass."

Digging deeper: Read Psalm 142. Who can we turn to when it seems nobody cares about us?

As a teen, I'm afraid I (Benny) gave my parents plenty to moan about. We were a respected, churchgoing family. Yet at age 14 I had already been convicted on several counts of grand larceny, including stealing my father's car. (Not the way to build a good relationship!) I had been given a three-year suspended sentence at a boys' penitentiary and was working at a fast-food restaurant to repay my father for court fees. My mother suffered, too. When she gave me money to sign up for a church youth retreat, I decided to invest it in a weekend of partying with my friends. The following Sunday, Mom discovered the truth when the youth leader mentioned I had been "missed" on the retreat. She was understandably hurt and frustrated.

> ❝ The companions of fools are suffering harm. Harm is showing up in the form of academic failure, preteen sex, drug abuse, vandalism, violence and suicide. Children are telling us they are lonely. One solution— for me, *the* solution—is to let our children walk with the two wise Christian companions God assigned them from the womb.[3] ❞
>
> —**Gregg Harris**

Though my parents loved me and worked hard to provide for me, I was ungrateful, cocky, and selfish. They should have challenged me. Instead, to keep peace in our home, they let me get away with a lot of things.

Think about Proverbs 29:17. If parents want peace in the home, what's the best way to get it?

I now have teenage children of my own, and by God's grace we enjoy a wonderful relationship. Yes, we have our share of misunderstandings. And, to be honest, we sometimes hurt and confuse one another. (One of my favorite sayings is, "Be patient with me...I've never been a father of teens before!") But Sheree and I worked hard to lay a foundation of acceptance and discipline during their early years, and now my oldest son Joshua says those words we have always hoped to hear: "I can talk to my parents about anything."

Anything?

His jump shot, our favorite football team, and whether Dad's tennis serve was in or out? All the time.

Fears and insecurities and goals and...girls? Yes. Not that we don't feel awkward at times. We do—but we talk anyway.

Sinful attitudes or comments? Yes. At his age, we're usually the one helping him assess his character, but sometimes he points out things in us.

This may be your experience, too. But for most parents and teens, such a close-knit relationship probably sounds like a fairy tale. We would expect some of those reading this study to say, "Are you living in a different century? It doesn't work that way anymore! Your kid may know how to do 'all the right things' when you're around, but one of these days you're in for a *big* surprise."

We don't think so, yet we can understand why a reader might be skeptical. So let's discuss it some more in the next section.

---

1 Is there anything you wish you could talk to your parents or teen about but haven't? If so, take a minute or two to fill in the blanks below. (You may want to use a separate sheet of paper.)

■ "I wish I could talk about _____ ."

■ "I haven't talked about it because _____

_____ ."

Who Says This Is "Normal"?

Let us ask a critical question: Why do we, as Christian parents and teens, accept the commonly-held idea that we're just not meant to get along? Has God said it's normal for families to fracture during the teen years? Does the Bible tell us kids will naturally rebel, and that parents are *supposed* to back off during adolescence?

No, on all counts. Nothing in the Bible or in the history of the church tells us that arguments, moodiness, and rebellion are a normal part of family life during the teenage years. The problem is quite simple: We've let the world, rather than God's Word, tell us what kind of role parents are to play.

Think about Proverbs 25:12. Do you value correction the way God does?

Many parents are caught off guard when their children reach age 12 or 13 and start to act "different." They develop a taste for music or friends or attitudes that Mom and Dad don't appreciate. All of a sudden, little Johnny is listening to heavy metal music, while Sally—who used to love having Mom tie bows in her hair—has decided to shave one side of her head. Not knowing how to respond, parents are easily intimidated. They don't like the changes, but they don't want to appear "too strict." So what do they do? Thinking their teens need more independence, they cut back on their oversight and involvement. Instead of showing their love through clear rules and consistent correction, they nag and complain and worry.

> **❝** By and large, modern parents, including Christians, have lost the notion of child-rearing as a purposeful activity in which they consciously and actively take the lead—especially through the children's teen years.[4] **❞**
>
> **—John Blattner**

Meanwhile, the teens aren't a bit confused. They have it all figured out. (At least they *think* they do!) And the first step is to put some distance between them and their parents. They begin an active search for acceptance among their peers. What Johnny and Sally usually overlook is the fact that their most vital relationships are not with those who see them only when they look and smell and act their best, but with those who see them at their worst…and love them anyway. Their greatest friends are those to whom God has given the wisdom and grace to help them fulfill their destiny.

Right. Dad and Mom.

Christian parents and teens are making a huge mistake if they let today's culture be the model for their relationship. The Bible warns us, "See to it that no one takes you captive through hollow and deceptive philosophy, which depends on human tradition and the basic principles of this world rather than on Christ" (Colossians 2:8). God has a better way! And he has described it for us in the Bible.

Digging deeper: What does Romans 12:2 mean when it says, "Do not conform any longer to the pattern of this world"?

We know that good parenting during the teen years requires flexibility, and that it's important to give a young adult more freedom. We're also aware teens need friends other than Dad and Mom. They will learn many lessons in maturity from these relationships. But what happens to those young men or women who are "let go" too early, and still need the loving, directive, maturity-forming oversight of their parents? Where, or with whom, or in what dangerous situation will they "find themselves"?

---

2 When is a teen is ready to be "let go"?

❏ When she gets her driver's license

❏ When he learns to sneak out the bedroom window

❏ When she reaches a certain age

❏ When his friends are all getting new freedoms

❏ When she is able to tie her own shoes

❏ When he or she is mature

We are deeply concerned that Christian families across America have been deceived by hollow and devastating myths about adolescence. This seems obvious when we read surveys which show that Christian and non-Christian teens have the same basic habits and attitudes about relationships, parental authority, and sex. And we ache every time we hear of miserable parents and miserable teens battling it out in the combat zone of their own home.

But as I've mentioned, the Bible tells us of a better way. And it's a practical way, even though it may seem strange at first. So without taking any more time, let's look at two of God's main guidelines for the parent/teen relationship: discipleship and "gatekeeping."

Go And Make Disciples!

Long before colleges and vocational schools were ever started, parents had a simple way of helping their children get ready for adulthood. Boys would work side by side with their fathers, or with some other skilled tradesman. Girls worked in the home with their mothers. Over the years they mastered the tasks, and were eventually able to live independently.

Not many parents today have jobs in which they can work side by side with their teens. But they can provide another kind of training which is far more important. They can give their children hands-on training in *character*. The word we use to describe that training is discipleship. It's kind of a big word, but the concept is easy to understand. We'll give you a couple of examples.

As a teenage guy, you might really admire the way a college athlete in your church plays—his technique or agility or speed. After watching him play at a church picnic, you ask for some pointers. (And even try to imitate some of his moves.)

Or as a girl, perhaps you look up to one of the older single women in your church. Her friendliness and warmth make her well-loved. And she has that balance of inner *and* outer beauty you desire as a Christian.

In both cases, you're being "discipled" by the individual you admire. If they are aware of your watching eyes, they may even want to get active in helping you out and coach you along in the areas where you want to improve. And, in time, they will impart to *you* the things that have helped them over the years.

With these examples of discipleship in mind, let's now look at the Bible's job description for *parents*: "Train a child in the way he should go, and when he is old he will not turn from it" (Proverbs 22:6). One definition of the word "train" as it's used in this verse is "to create a thirst." It suggests deliberate, highly purposeful leadership. In other words, it means discipleship.

Digging deeper: Read 2 Corinthians 6:14-17. Does God expect Christians to be like everybody else?

Teenagers are "thirsty" for acceptance, friendship, and guidance. (Admit it, teens—you're not really perfect yet, are you? You still need guidance!) Either parents will quench this thirst, or the teen will turn to others for companionship and advice. In case you're wondering, it's rare to find a teen mature enough to quench this thirst solely through a relationship with God. Our years of working in youth ministry and now parenting teens has convinced us that *independence* from parents does not create *dependence* on God.

During a child's early years, discipleship comes quite naturally for parents. Dads can't wait to show their sons how to swing a baseball bat; moms enjoy helping their daughters feed their dolls. Christian parents are usually conscientious about teaching their children how to answer the phone, share with friends, pick up their toys, and all the rest. But it's during the teenage years, when most parents think their training is over, that discipleship is most urgent. Parental discipleship should grow stronger, not weaker, during adolescence! What's more important for your son, hitting home runs or learning to control his temper when he strikes out? And why teach your daughter to burp a doll without imparting the biblical value of motherhood?

> ❝ A family run on 'democratic lines' with all members, children as well as adults, considered equal would be unnatural...'One child, one vote,' is a formula for the end of the family.[6] ❞
>
> —Dr. Michael Platt

Some parents assume this kind of training isn't necessary, or that it would make teens overly dependent. Actually, it does just the opposite. Effective discipleship helps teens gain the character, skill, and confidence to succeed in their relationships and careers. Also, by making the time and effort to teach their children essential Christian doctrines, parents lay the foundation for a lifelong walk with God. (There are several good resources for this, depending on your child's maturity level. You'll find some recommendations at the end of Study Eight.)

---

3 Which of the following would a good coach do for his or her athletes? (Check all that apply, then circle the ones you think parents should do for their teens.)

❏ Keep an eye on their schedule

❏ Warn about bad habits

❏ Understand when they're lazy

❏ Push them toward excellence

❏ Encourage constantly

❏ Be patient but persistent

❏ Help them set goals

❏ Accept poor performance

Digging deeper: Can you see the two extremes of parenting shown in Proverbs 13:24 and Ephesians 6:4?

We parents tend to lean toward two extremes during our kids' teenage years. Some of us try to overpower our children and make them act a certain way; some of us let our teens do whatever they want, convinced that making foolish mistakes is an unavoidable part of growing up. Either way, the teen suffers and the gap between parent and teen widens.

Let us be very clear. Dad and Mom, you're not supposed to be tyrants but you are the boss. Teen…you're not the boss. It's as simple as that.

Mentors And Memories

Jesus is our model of discipleship. He and his disciples spent the better part of three years together, much of which was spent talking. Jesus had a lot to say and only a little time to say it. (Parents, time flies so fast, doesn't it? By the teen years, we only have a little time left, too.) Jesus shared his heart with them. He strongly but lovingly rebuked them when they needed it. He answered their questions—even the really bright ones like, "So, which one of us is gonna get the best seat in heaven?" He also showed them the road to true greatness—servanthood— by washing their feet and cooking their breakfast on the

During adolescence, young people face internal conflicts about their worth and identity. We parents have the privilege of guiding our sons and daughters successfully through these years. The task demands skillful leadership and a biblical understanding of parental authority. But it also requires visible expressions of love. To help stimulate your creativity, here are some of the special things we've done to show our affection for our teens.

■ Surprising Josh by re-scheduling a meeting so that Dad could be at the basketball game. (An out-of-town trip had caused us to miss one, and Josh had said, "It's just not the same when you're not there.")

■ Arranging for surprise overnighters with friends who just "show up" to spend the night. (The kitchen has usually been well-stocked that afternoon, too!)

■ Arranging for Jaime's close friend—who now lives in another state—to come to her 13th birthday party. When Jaime opened her eyes and saw Megan with a bow on her head, she was wonderfully surprised.

■ Finding an encouraging card to give Josh during a season when many of our conversations seemed to be focusing on areas of needed change in his life.

■ Letting them wear the shirt, shoes, earrings, or suit we had planned to wear that day. (How can they possibly be old enough to wear our things?)

■ Buying Josh a roomy bag to carry all his "stuff" for his first high school game (filled with bags of his favorite goodies and gum to share on the bus ride with his teammates).

beach. And yet there was never any question about who held the position of authority.

It took some time, but the disciples eventually realized how much they needed their Master's input. Teens, you also need input—from your parents. They aren't perfect like Jesus is, but turn to them anyway. If a teen who wants to succeed in life doesn't recognize his or her need for help, there's a real problem. We've never met anyone who woke up at age 25 mature...responsible... able to make wise decisions ...full of godly character. Those who develop these qualities get lots of input along the way.

Single parents obviously face a bigger challenge, especially when raising a child of the opposite sex. Can a mom disciple her teenage son or a dad his teenage daughter? In many ways, yes. You may want to involve others in the process. But *your* influence is still the most important one. The time you spend together building your relationship and making memories will go a long way in helping your teen develop godly character.

Parents, please don't think you have to be perfect to disciple your children. (We certainly aren't!) What you need most are devotion, discernment, and patience. Lots of patience. Teens, it may take you awhile to see how much you need your parents' training. That will come

Think about Luke 14:11. Here's one strategy for success the world will never teach you!

through lots of talking and laughing and being together. With God's help, you will become more humble and teachable (key qualities for success) as your parents grow in wisdom and unselfishness (so they can train you in the way you *should* go, not just the way they want you to go).

Mother To Daughter. I (Sheree) really enjoy my relationship with my teenage daughter, Jaime. Our favorite pasttimes are talking and shopping. (Hey, we can do them both at the same time!)

Discipling her involves some structured things like reading and discussing materials together. But it mostly involves just sharing my life with her in normal, everyday situations. Cooking and cleaning together. Practicing basketball defenses in the living room for her upcoming game—things I only know because Josh first showed *me*! Crying together during sad or touching moments of a movie. Talking about ways she needs to grow in character or take her responsibilities more seriously.

Sharing time—and lots of it—is an important aspect of discipleship in the home. For it's during the daily, unplanned events that I am teaching my daughter how to respond to real-life situations. From *me* she is learning how to manage her time. Respond to interruptions and inconveniences. Respect her future husband. Care for a home and children. (Gulp… Jesus, how I need your help!)

Father To Son. For several years Joshua and I (Benny) have shared breakfast on Saturday mornings. I look forward to these times to talk with him about his week, his relationship with God, tomorrow's football game, and just about anything on his or my heart. Sometimes we'll discuss a book or theological article I've asked him to read.

WHERE DO WE BEGIN?

Though we've used the terms "teacher" and "student," discipleship isn't meant to be like an algebra class or a European History exam. Instead, think of it as a journey—a relaxed walk down the interesting road of life.

If you're already on the road, the following questions will give you some good things to talk about. If you haven't started yet—and especially if your relationship is tense right now—these should help convince you discipleship is a trip worth taking.

What's positive about our relationship right now? What's negative?

What do I admire most about my parent/teen?

In what areas do I need to know my parent/teen better?

What in me would need to change for discipling to work?

Do we need someone to help us sort through past problems in order to make a fresh start in our relationship?

But as good as these times have been, my favorite memory is the weekend trip we took several years ago on his 13th birthday. Another father and son, Mark and Andy Walker, joined us. (Josh and Andy are close friends and were born just six days apart. Josh wants you to know he's the oldest!) We ate and played and laughed together for a long time. And then we dads talked about our past. Mistakes we had made. How we came to know Jesus. Our passion for being involved in the local church.

We also talked about how our sons needed to develop their own convictions and passions. And as the evening ended, we prayed with them that their love for God would deepen during the teen years. That rather than fritter their years away, they would discover and fulfill his call on their lives.

Nothing forced. Just dads and sons being together, sharing our lives and hearts at a time when most start pulling away from each other.

I'll remember that weekend as long as I live. And I think Josh will, too.

 Parents and teens, what's the best memory you have of time spent together? What made it special?

Guarding The Gate

Imagine this situation, teens. It's 6:00 p.m. on a Friday night. As you're looking out the window, you see a black car pull up to your house. A strange man gets out, puts a gift-wrapped box on your doorstep, then speeds away.

You open the door to take a closer look and see a bright neon tag on the package. It has your name on it! With growing excitement, you start peeling off the ribbon and paper...

At the same moment your dad pulls into the driveway. But you're not watching him—you're about to pull the lid off the box.

Suddenly he jerks you off your feet, drags you inside, and slams the door. Has he gone crazy? Did he have a bad day at work? Why would he spoil your surprise?

And then outside the door you hear a loud explosion.

The Old Testament tells us about a group of people known as gatekeepers who had the job of protecting the temple (1 Chronicles 9:17-27). It was their duty to make sure nothing unholy was taken *into* the temple, and that nothing holy was taken *out* of the temple.

Several years ago we heard a man describe parents as "gatekeepers." But rather than guard a building, they guard their children. His point made a lasting impact on us. Moms and dads should be vigilant to make sure nothing harmful comes *into* their children, and that nothing good is stolen *from* them. In other words, parents are on full alert. When they see something that puts their child at risk, they don't just stand by to watch what happens. They rush to the rescue.

Usually it's not bombs on the doorstep that parents have to worry about. But what about raunchy rap lyrics, suggestive sitcoms, or the kid next door whose language should be rated X? Unless they're deaf, dumb, and blind, loving parents won't let this kind of garbage through the gate. Instead, they take the time to read the lyrics. Preview the movies. Meet the friends. They carefully monitor the things that influence their children. And when they see something dangerous, they don't hesitate for a minute to bar the gate.

Now let's be honest. Unless teens see the need for having a gatekeeper, it won't be long until they are seriously upset with Mom and Dad. Few teens *enjoy* getting their parents' advice on hair styles, skirt length, or music collections. That's why the average parent lacks the courage to get involved on this level. He or she doesn't want to be labeled as "overprotective" for "depriving" a child of "memorable experiences."

Parents, it may seem easier to leave the gate unguarded than to risk conflict with your teen. It's easy to convince

> 44 Being a parent doesn't mean being an ogre or a relentless disciplinarian. Rather it means asserting ourselves as adults who have more experience, knowledge, and skill than our offspring. Children and teenagers are young and inexperienced. They very much need and want guidance and instruction from us.[7]
>
> —**David Elkind**

Think about 1 Peter 5:8-9. What would the devil like to do to teens? How can parents prevent it?

yourself that relaxing the standards a little now and then won't do any harm. But it will. Let me (Benny) tell you a little more about my own childhood, and I think you'll see my point.

I grew up attending church meetings every Sunday. My father was a leader in the church, and as a young boy I had a desire to know and follow God. Yet, as I mentioned earlier, by age 14 I was a convicted criminal.

What happened?

Like many other "Christian" teens today, I was living a double life. My parents insisted I go to church meetings on Sundays, and I did—but only after joining some friends for a cigarette behind the building. I made sure just enough of my weekly allowance was left over from weekend partying to drop my tithe in the offering plate. And I didn't even see my hypocrisy the night I argued with a girl at a party about whether faith or works saved you—while holding a beer in one hand and a cigarette in the other.

Both my parents and I had a serious problem. We all thought I was just "going through a phase"—you know, trying to come to grips with my beliefs and identity. But the only grip that came was that of the police officer who finally nailed me for a stolen car incident. After my third appearance in juvenile court, when the judge said I would serve time if I so much as skipped school, my parents and I woke up. Something had to change.

The changes were major. I starting working long hours to pay fines, which made me too tired to party. To get my grades up in school, I joined the choir. (None of my rowdy friends dared follow me there!) I even started attending a Bible study led by a football teammate…and that's where I found the relationship with Jesus that changed the course of my life. I went on to become a pastor. Believe it or not, the same juvenile judge who sentenced me became one of the leaders of my church in its early years!

Did my parents see the danger signs in those early teenage years? I'm sure they did. But I was so headstrong they had little hope of influencing me.

Digging deeper: If you want to read about two preacher's kids who really lived a double life, see 1 Samuel 2:12-17, 22-25; 4:10-11.

Did *I* see the warning signals—so subtle at first—that I was running away from my parents and God? No. I saw myself as a pretty good kid. In fact, I was proud that I wasn't as wild as a lot of my friends.

The seeds of compromise take root deep below the surface. And like myself, most teens become masters at hiding from their parents. Meanwhile, too many parents cope with the bad attitudes and behavior by looking the other way, hoping and praying their teen will eventually turn out okay (as if "okay" were an acceptable standard for the authentic Christian teenager).

We don't want to give the impression that parents are always right and teens are always wrong about movies, music, friends, and everything else. We know some young people who make very wise choices. But who is best equipped and most responsible for sniffing out the garbage that gets dumped at the gate? The Bible is clear: God gives *parents* the mandate and the grace to protect their children—especially in the teen years—from anything or anyone that might hurt their relationship with God. As former President Harry Truman once said, "The buck stops here."

---

5 *Warning: Answering this question honestly may prove hazardous to your pride.*

Teen: Describe one time you got mad at your parents for not letting you do something...then later you realized they had done the right thing.

Parent: Describe one time you kept your teen from doing something...then later realized you had made a mistake.

Think about Proverbs 4:10-13. Listening to parents may not seem "cool," but it sure is smart!

Teens, by now you probably realize that your parents are less than perfect. They make mistakes. They fail. They overreact to you, sometimes out of fear but usually because of love. Be patient with them.

And parents, you need to be patient, too. Sure your daughter wants to pick her own friends, and your son tells you life today is different than when you were a kid. Sure they think they know it all. (Didn't you?) But don't assume they stay up late every night planning new ways to drive you crazy.

> ❝ There is no reason for the parent/teen years to be characterized by rebellion and mutual hostility. I am convinced that by the time you have weathered pierced ears and paper routes…Sunday morning battles for the bathroom and Sunday night term papers, you and your high-school graduate can part as friends who want to see each other again as often as possible.[9] ❞
>
> **—Dr. Robert Laurent**

There will always be disagreements and misunderstandings. As Dr. James Dobson says, "Parenting isn't for cowards." Neither is being a godly teenager who dares to buck the tide of compromise and be a role model for his or her peers.

But with the right perspective and a soft heart, families can draw closer during the adolescent years. As parents, we must fully embrace—and reestablish if necessary—the authority God has given us in the life of our teen. Love "always protects," even when that protection isn't wanted (1 Corinthians 13:7). As teens, you must trust your parents' judgment more than you trust your own. Remember, you have an enemy who seeks to steal your passion for God and turn you against the people who love you most.

By telling parents to back off while telling teens to "do your own thing," today's experts have ruined what God meant to be a great relationship. But we're not going along with it. We've seen what happens when parents and teens treat one another with love and respect. We know it's possible for moms and dads to be best friends with their children without giving up their role as gatekeeper and teacher. And we are proud to point out those brave young men and women who have the character to walk in their parents' footsteps rather than follow the crowd.

Working side by side, a new generation of parents and teens is enjoying God's best for the family. It can happen in your home, too. ■

1. Do you lean toward either of the parenting extremes mentioned on page 42?

2. "Parental discipleship," says the author, "should grow stronger, not weaker, during adolescence." Do you agree?

3. What are the biggest dangers your teen is currently facing? (If it's bombs on the doorstep, you may want to consider a different neighborhood!)

4. After reading this study, do you feel you are giving your teen (A) Too little freedom, (B) Too much freedom, or (C) The right amount of freedom?

1. How do you respond when your parents say "no" to a request?

2. How would you rate your parents? (A) Too strict, (B) Too easy, or (C) Just right

3. List two or three weak spots in your life where you see a need for your parents' training.

4. Do you trust your parents enough to live by their rules? (Remember—athletes obey their coaches because they know it's good for them.)

5. How would you approach your parents if you felt they didn't understand you?

1. Do you find it easy or hard to admit when you're wrong? Why?

2. What are your expectations of the teen years?

3. Share your answers to Question 4 on page 45.

4. How is your relationship different from the world's model for parents and teens? Where is it similar?

5. How can you work together to "guard the gate"?

Answer to Warm-Up (from page 35): Within weeks after entering coach Bela Karolyi's training program, Mary Lou was screaming mad over his demands. She made her "big leap" when she finally learned to trust his opinions more than her own. "I'd finally realized that you had to give him the best...The whole idea was to get a routine so that it was good enough for Bela, because if it was, it would be good enough for anybody." Thanks to Karolyi, it was good enough for the gold. (Source: *Mary Lou: Creating An Olympic Champion*, McGraw-Hill Book Company, ©1986, p. 82)

DO YOU DARE TO BE DIFFERENT?

BIBLE STUDY   Proverbs 1:29-33

WARM-UP   Norway lemmings are small rodents best-known for their mass migrations. When they are on the move (and they can travel nine miles in a day), they won't let anything stand in their way. Entire herds will plunge into a lake or an ocean—even though it means almost certain death.

Why do they do it?

A. Because it's cool

B. Because of the *Rockin' Rodents* song, "Sink or Swim"

C. Because migrating makes them hot and sweaty

D. Because they are looking for somewhere to nest

E. Because they have brains the size of a pea

(See page 65 for answer)

PERSONAL STUDY   As a little girl, Susan was compliant and cheerful. Like all toddlers, she had her challenging days when she seemed to test all of Dad's and Mom's rules. Yet her favorite things to do were helping Mom around the house. Running to meet Dad when he came home from work. And going to Sunday meetings with the church.

She loved picnics with the family, spending the night with friends from the church, and picking out her own clothes to wear (even though they often didn't match). But she *didn't* like scary movies. And when Corrie, her teen-aged cousin, argued with her parents, Susan got very upset. In fact, she didn't really enjoy visiting Corrie's house because of all the yelling and door-slamming.

As Susan approached her teen years, though, things began to change. Friendships in school became more important than those in the church. She started complaining about not having the "right" clothes, and suddenly wanted a hairstyle just like her best friend, Tammy. She started spending more time on the phone than helping Mom around the house. She greeted Dad from work only when he came and found her—usually on her bed wearing earphones. School activities started crowding out youth group events and picnics with the family.

And getting up early on Sunday mornings took forever!

Susan's favorite TV shows—you know, the ones *everybody* watched—featured lots of romance and obnoxious parents. (She even caught an occasional soap opera when Mom was out running errands in the afternoon.)

At first, Susan's parents weren't really concerned. After all, they reasoned, don't all teenagers go through these kinds of "adjustments"? Besides, Susan was still getting decent grades in school. Didn't drink or take drugs. Kept her Bible on her bedside table.

Then the arguments started. And Susan didn't notice she was starting to sound a lot like cousin Corrie.

"You actually want to *meet* my basketball coach before the practices start? How embarrassing!"

"Come on, Mom. Everybody wears this. You can't expect me to dress like a little girl anymore."

"No, I don't want to invite kids from the church to my party. They won't...you know...fit in with my friends from school."

> **❝** It is easier to give in [to teens]. But we pay an inordinate price for such giving in. Teenagers will fight limits and rules and may say things to the effect that the parent is a bad person, old-fashioned, unfeeling, et cetera. But at a deeper level teenagers know that the parent has risked this out of caring, and they appreciate it.[1] **❞**
>
> —David Elkind

"Gimme a break, Dad. What's wrong with my music? You complain about anything that sounds different from the stuff you and Mom lister. to."

"This is ridiculous! Mike and I are just going out to a movie. You'd think I was eloping or something!"

Although they felt uneasy, Susan's parents backed off. Trying to talk with her just created more tension. She would accuse them of treating her like a child. Sometimes Dad yelled back. Mom often cried.

It was a lot easier to let her have her way.

Think about Proverbs 3:7 and 26:12. The wisest teen is the one who seeks out the wisdom of others.

What's Best For Your Teen?

Some of you know firsthand what Susan and her parents were going through. If so, we have some suggestions many parents and teens have found helpful in straightening out these kinds of problems.

But we've got to be honest with you. The solutions aren't easy. Families like Susan's often start well but finish poorly because parents lack the courage to hang in there when the going gets tough.

Some react. Yell. Threaten. Criticize. Coerce. Nag. Slap. Others choose to withdraw. Gripe. Become bitter. Give up. Make excuses. Assume "it's just a phase."

But few parents have the guts to lead their teens without compromise. It's the rare family that has a Dad and Mom who command respect, require obedience, and exercise authority—all without harshness or anger. Why? Because most don't want to risk being misunderstood by their teen as too strict or overly protective.

And yet guess which families come through the teen years most successfully?

---

1 Which of these would you consider acceptable "phases" of childhood or adolescence?

❏ The "Give me something to chew, I'm teething!" phase

❏ The "I smell something funny in my diaper" phase

❏ The "Girls are disgusting, boys are gross" phase

❏ The "I'm old enough to make my own decisions" phase

❏ The "Everybody in my family is a jerk but me" phase

❏ The "But nose rings are the *ultimate!*" phase

❏ The "Mom, can I spend the week at the mall?" phase

Digging deeper: Read Philippians 1:9-11. This was Paul's prayer for the Philippians—and it's an excellent way for parents to pray for their teens.

As we saw in Study Three, God's plan for parenting in the teenage years hinges on gatekeeping and discipleship—in short, becoming more involved rather than less involved during the season between childhood and adulthood. And yes, that takes a level of commitment many parents seem to lack.

But discipleship and gatekeeping require more than courage. They require *discernment*: the ability to evaluate the positive or negative influence of a particular person or activity. Discernment requires seeing things and people with God's eyes, and then being willing to make a wise decision about what you've seen. Even if your decision is unpopular.

As parents we must discern those things which could influence our children negatively. And then, by pointing those things out to our teens, we are training them to be discerning as well—even if they aren't initially thrilled to follow our leadership.

Here's an example that is still fresh in our minds.

On a recent weekend afternoon, Josh and Jaime wanted to go with some friends to a local recreation center to play basketball. They thought they had it all worked out. One of the other moms would drive and swim in the indoor pool while they played in the gym. Knowing we didn't have any family plans, they were already dressed in basketball gear when they came in our room to ask if they could go.

Digging deeper: Read Proverbs 4:20-22. Sometimes it may seem like your parents' discipline or rules will kill you, but they won't. What will they do?

The other two parents had already given permission for their sons. But we were unsettled.

First, we explained, it sure made it hard to say "no" with them standing before us in shorts and warm-up suits with transportation already arranged. From now on, we said, don't make plans until we talk.

Second, we had always required in situations like this that an adult be present to supervise any awkward moments. A mom swimming laps in the pool down the hall wasn't exactly "supervision."

Are our kids in elementary school? No. They're in high school. Did they eagerly accept our hesitation? No. Although they didn't blatantly argue, they had questions.

> 66 I am not proposing that parents become totalitarian dictators, manipulating their children's lives like puppets on a string, prescribing and proscribing behavior at every turn. What I am proposing is *training*: training those who are naive and inexperienced so that they gain wisdom and confidence; training those who are dependent so that they may provide for themselves; in short, training children so that they may reach adulthood.[2] 99
>
> —**John Blattner**

They didn't understand. They wondered when they *will* be able to go to a recreation center or mall without supervision.

Ouch! Comments like these can easily knock the wind out of parents. It would be so much easier to give in. Even as we talked we *sounded* overprotective. Yet we couldn't do it. Our instincts said "no."

Was it because we don't trust our teens? Were we worried they would come home two hours later with pink mohawks and safety pins in their cheeks, spewing profanities? No. It's just that we've learned to trust the voice inside that cautions us about situations like these. Christian parents will not always be able to put their finger on a specific chapter and verse that supports their decisions. Though they should have clear, biblical principles for their parenting, they often need supernatural assistance from the Holy Spirit.

Maybe the gym would have been nearly empty. Or the guys who happened to be there were great guys with excellent court attitudes. That wasn't the point. At this stage in their lives, we just don't feel comfortable dropping our kids off in such situations. We have seen where such freedoms can lead, and that's not where we want our teens to wind up.

How To Stop "Stupid" Habits From Starting

We'll finish the story in a minute, but first this side note from early childhood. Suppose you're watching a cartoon video with your toddler, and he hears one character call the other "stupid." Soon, you notice him talking about that "stupid" truck with the wheel that fell off or the "stupid" way a neighbor girl wears her hair.

In four years he had never used the word. And yet after watching that one movie a few times, "stupid" is a daily part of his vocabulary. Months later you're still attempting to rid him of it.

Toddlers aren't the only ones quick to pick up bad habits. Teens are just as easily influenced (if not more so) by those around them. A wise parent screens movies for his or her toddler, pointing out wrong speech or negative attitudes. Those parents who *remain* wise stay involved as their children get older, and continue training their teens how to recognize and avoid harmful influences.

Think about Proverbs 13:24. How can you tell whether a parent loves or hates a child?

To make this more personal, parents, let us ask you some questions. Who do you want teaching your son self-control on the basketball court when he misses a shot or gets unjustly called for a foul? Who is best able to train your daughter to handle herself appropriately around the guys? Who will be modeling for your teen things like respect for adults? Encouragement? Servanthood?

The unsupervised toddler never hears that "stupid" is an inappropriate, selfish word. So he imitates it. Likewise, an adolescent who regularly hangs out in unsupervised situations with peers doesn't learn that yelling at the referee or flirting with the guys is unacceptable. In fact, those peers become his or her "disciplers" and role models. No wonder Dad and Mom soon start seeing the negative effects at home.

55

2 In the space below, give at least one example of how you've been "discipled" (that is, heavily influenced) by your peers. (Parents, you may want to pick an example from your teenage years…if you can think back that far!)

_____

Now, back to Josh and Jaime's request to play basketball. We talked with them for quite a while, explaining our concerns and listening to theirs. Bottom line? We decided it was still premature to put them into the situation without an adult who could handle the potential consequences.

So I (Benny) got up from a potential afternoon nap, changed my clothes, and took Josh, Jaime, and friends to the recreation center. Not to "babysit" them or clear the gym of any "negative influences," but to be there in case there was a need for dialogue. Or attitudes needed to be adjusted. Or tempers started to flare. Or the game simply got too rough. (Speaking of rough…I was sore for days after trying to keep up with all those young guys!)

As it turned out, the supervision probably wasn't needed. No major issues surfaced in the gym that day. The games were pretty rough, but more because of the beating we took than because of the attitudes or language of the other players. And yet you never know when that incident with long-term negative consequences will occur.

Many parents would rather take the risk than pay the price. As for us, we'd prefer to reach the end of the movie and find we didn't "need" to watch it than spend the next six months dealing with "stupid."

Think about Proverbs 12:1. Here's one case where "stupid" is the only appropriate word!

Freedom…At Any Price?

We've talked to plenty of parents who are uncomfortable with this level of oversight. They would argue—and often quite convincingly—that young people need more and more freedom as they mature, and that too much supervision could stunt a teen's development.

We agree. Learning to handle freedom is a vital part of growing up. Yet when freedom is given too soon or too quickly, it can have disastrous consequences.

We were doing a seminar for parents in another city when we spoke with the mother of a young teenage son. (We'll call him Brad.) The family was actively involved in the church. Brad was involved in the youth ministry and had enjoyed a strong relationship with the Lord since childhood.

Like many teens, Brad had developed an interest in basketball. During the summer break from school he developed a casual friendship with some of the neighborhood guys. A few of them played basketball regularly at the neighborhood courts.

When Brad first started asking about playing with the guys, his parents were hesitant. They had no problem letting Brad invite friends over to their home, but they were concerned about Brad being with them regularly in unsupervised situations. They had noticed these guys hanging around the neighborhood and were concerned about their potential influence on Brad.

Later they realized their instincts were right. But at the time, they assumed Brad's complaints might be valid. Maybe they were being "too strict," and just needed to lighten up like he said. So finally they agreed to let Brad play once a week.

> **"** Until my children are old and wise enough to distinguish their enemies from their friends, I hold the responsibility to conduct both a defense and an offense on their behalf, demonstrating all the time how and why it is done for their benefit.[3] **"**
>
> —**Gordon MacDonald**

This was fine with him…at first. After a few games, though, he started complaining.

"Mom and Dad, they're really nice guys. Besides, there's nothing else to do. What's a few more hours a week gonna hurt? Come on. I'm almost 14 years old!" he pleaded.

Brad's parents, like most parents of teens, lacked confidence. Soon they began to question their discernment. Perhaps Brad *was* ready for more freedoms with friends. He would benefit from the exercise. And who knows? Maybe some opportunities for evangelism would come up with some of the guys. He sure would be more pleasant around the house if they allowed more basketball.

Brad was thrilled. But within a few weeks his parents started noticing the changes. More requests to be with his new friends. Disrespectful attitudes. Arguments. Larger

Think about Proverbs 29:15. What becomes of a teen left to himself or herself without parental oversight?

blocks of time alone in his room. Angry outbursts when they said no to his requests.

By the time we spoke with Brad's mom, she was very concerned. School had started so there was no time for daily basketball games. But Brad's disrespectful attitudes and sour disposition remained. "It doesn't matter how much freedom we give him," she said. "It's never enough. The more we let him do, the more he wants." Only six months earlier things had been going well. Now their relationship was strained and uncomfortable.

3 Take a minute or two to give the following some serious thought.

Teen: Is there any area where you feel you should be given more freedom? Less freedom?

Parent: Is there any area where you feel your teen should have more freedom? Less freedom?

Blameless And Innocent

In case you're wondering how far we plan to go with this, relax. We aren't recommending that young people spend their teen years in a protective bubble, secluded from the evils of the world around them. We don't have coils of barbed wire around our house or strict rules that say no non-Christian friends. No movies or TV. No radios that receive transmissions from non-Christian stations. No basketball with the neighborhood kids. And certainly no relationships with the opposite sex!

We can't seclude our teens. But we do want to protect their innocence in a society that is hostile toward the things of God and full of worldly distractions. Exercising discernment and maintaining our children's innocence doesn't just protect them *from* the world. It prepares them *for* the world!

Teens, as you spend time with worldly peers you are regularly exposed to profanity. Sensual dress. Flirtatious behavior. Disrespectful attitudes toward teachers or parents. Competition for attention or a date to the homecoming dance. Sarcastic, critical comments about other teens. At first these things may shock you. But over time they become less offensive—even acceptable.

Soon, you don't notice the profanity as much. And then in a moment of frustration that four-letter word just pops out of your mouth.

You realize *all* the kids wear attention-getting clothes, and soon you're frustrated with your parents because they're so old-fashioned about what you can buy.

> ❝ Youth are a vulnerable lot. They lack the wisdom and discernment that experience of life often brings. They are dismayingly prone to making heroes out of idiots.[4] ❞
>
> —**Michael Keating**

You start to see that the girls who flirt always get the best-looking guys. And slowly you realize you act differently around the guys at school than the guys in the church (especially when your parents are around).

Listen up, and listen well. Do you know what happens to a razor blade if you bang it repeatedly with a rock? It becomes dull. And that's just what has happened to your conscience. You have given in to worldliness. You have let what others think and do influence you more than biblical principles. You have chosen to imitate the conduct, appearance, and values of non-Christians rather than being courageous enough to obey God.

God doesn't want you to waste your life on the world. He has called you to be blameless. Parents, as our teens mature, we can expect them to stand up and even speak out against these kinds of worldly pressures. *But it takes training in discernment.* And few are getting it. In fact, many young people have dulled their consciences before even reaching their teenage years.

Webster's Dictionary defines the word blameless as "being free from accusation or fault." It suggests the kind of pure living that makes teens mature, able to lead and influence their peers instead of being led and influenced by them. Blameless teens are those who haven't grown up too fast. Their innocence has been maintained by wise and discerning parents.

This kind of innocence can, at times, make a godly teen seem naive. Some time ago I (Benny) used the term "reefer" during a Sunday morning message. Most in the

Think about Acts 24:16. How do you think Paul went about accomplishing this?

59

ARE YOU WALKING IN THE WAYS OF THE WORLD?

Every family needs to develop its own standards regarding worldliness and innocence. As you pray, God will show you specific areas to assess. To help you get started, here are three of the most common signs that a teen is being molded by the world. Do you detect any of these symptoms?

Peer Conformity

- Imitating whatever the youth culture says is "in" or "cool."
- Choosing hair and clothing styles on the basis of what's "popular" rather than personal taste.
- Compromising personal standards in order to fit in.

Dwindling Spiritual Health

- Lack of interest in church involvement.
- Little or no personal pursuit of God (prayer, Bible study, and so on).
- "Hands in your pockets" worship.

Withdrawal From Positive Christian Influences

- Eagerness to spend a lot of time with non-Christian peers.
- Embarrassment about having Christian friends and a Christian family.
- Listening to or watching unwholesome entertainment.

Digging deeper: Read 1 Timothy 1:18-19. What can happen if you don't hold on to a good conscience?

congregation laughed, especially those of us who grew up in the '60s. But I couldn't help noticing that many of the teens didn't laugh. Rather, they looked a little puzzled. That's when I realized they had never heard this term.

Though I paused to explain what the word meant, I found the experience encouraging. There was something refreshing about seeing teenagers who weren't aware of something so familiar to my generation when we were their age. (In fact, a little too familiar to many of us!)

Some would suggest this kind of "naivete" is unhealthy. After all, don't teens need to understand and even experience certain things to be aware of the potential dangers? And certainly they need to be able to relate to their non-Christian friends and not be thought of as nerds or geeks. How can they possibly evangelize their peers if they are so obviously "separate" from them—confined to their insulated Christian world by overprotective parents? This is a pivotal question, and it deserves a careful answer. For us, though, the Bible leaves no room for debate: Wisdom and maturity aren't best gained by "trial and error." "This assumption," writes Professor David Elkind, "rests on the mistaken belief that a bad experience is the best preparation for a bad experience. In fact, just the reverse is true: *a good experience is the best preparation for a bad experience.*"[5] The most mature teens we know across this country are those who have had the least contact with things of this world and the most contact with the things of God. They have learned to "fear" (respect and obey) their parents. As young adults, they now fear God. And that's the safest, most direct route to wisdom (Proverbs 1:8).

4 In which of the following situations would it be wise to insist on your way rather than following advice?

❑ Driving: Your instructor tells you to stay in the right-hand lane; you find the left lane more exciting

❑ Academics: Your teacher assigns a book report on *Moby Dick*; you would prefer to do "Show and Tell" using your postcards from Sea World

❑ Flying: Your instructor tells you to ease back on the throttle; you want to slam it forward

❑ Medicine: Your doctor prescribes an antibiotic; you're convinced Milk Duds would be more effective

❑ Becoming An Adult: Your parents encourage you to work part-time; you would rather join a rock band

Practice Makes Perfect

Learning the fear of the Lord is critical for teens. Look at this powerful passage (sprinkled with some of our comments) from Proverbs 1:29-33, which gives us both a warning and a promise:

Digging deeper: Read Proverbs 23:17 and 24:19-20. It may look like worldly teens are having a good time, but they are headed for big trouble.

Since they hated knowledge and did not choose *[notice, teens, it's your choice]* to fear the Lord, since they would not accept my advice *[which often comes through parents and other authority figures]* and spurned my rebuke *[that means rejecting correction and discipline]*, they will eat the fruit of their ways and be filled with the fruit of their schemes *[in other words, eventually your sin catches up to you]*. For the waywardness of the simple *[meaning the unwise]* will kill them *[destroy their usefulness to God and perhaps even their lives]*, and the complacency *[apathetic, "what's the big deal" attitude]* of fools will destroy them; but whoever listens to me *[again, God often speaks to teens through their parents]* will live in safety and be at ease, without fear of harm.

(You should probably read this a few times. It's good stuff and God has some things to say to you through it.) So how can we avoid the dangers shown in this proverb?

You've heard it said that "practice makes perfect." What teens "practice" in their relationship with their parents they will eventually "perfect" in their relationship with God. Those who practice respect, obedience, and right attitudes toward their parents will have a similar response to God.

The opposite, however, will also be true. Those who resist, resent, or only comply outwardly with their parents (while they're watching) will inevitably suffer in their walk with God.

> **"** In today's society we seem unable to accept the fact of adolescence, that there are young people in transition from childhood to adulthood who need adult guidance and direction. Rather, we assume the teenager is a kind of adult. Whether we confer premature adulthood upon teenagers because we are too caught up in our own lives to give them the time and attention they require or because we feel helpless to provide them with the safe world they need, the end result is the same: teenagers have no place in this society.[6] **"**
>
> **—David Elkind**

That's why *today* matters. And tonight when Mom says it's time to finish your homework. And Friday when Dad says you can't use the car. The habits you're creating now will follow you. Your future relationships—with a spouse, children, friends, and the Lord—are being shaped today by the way you respond to your parents.

Think about Proverbs 15:10 and 19:16.
Resisting your parents' instruction is like committing spiritual suicide!

We know it's not cool to be seen as naive and "different." A girl rarely becomes the homecoming queen because of her modesty or outspoken Christian commitment. And when is the last time the guy who leads the school Bible study and treats the girls with gentlemanly respect was elected "most likely to succeed"? But you have to be different in order to make a difference. And that is what God has called you to do.

Teens, until you learn to discern those things that can slowly twist you from godly standards to worldly desires... trust your parents. They've lived longer. They've paid the price for certain mistakes, and they want to spare you that pain. They don't always know *why* they feel what they feel, so don't always demand answers. (Sometimes it's just an impression from the Holy Spirit.) And even though it may not always seem this way, they have your best interests at heart. They've learned that popularity with your friends isn't nearly as important as your growth in God.

And, yes, they make mistakes. But that's between them and God. If you do your part by respecting and obeying them, God will certainly reward you.

---

5 Describe a situation when it was hard for you to trust your parents' judgment, but it turned out for the best. (Another chance to walk down "Memory Lane," parents!)

Whatever It Takes

You've probably noticed this study has had a lot to say to parents. This was deliberate. Learning to discern must begin with us. Only then can we help our young men and women attain their full potential in God.

And it begins with a "reality check" in our own lives. Can we train our teens to be discerning about their friends and movies and music if we compromise in these areas ourselves? Can we really expect to command their respect when they see us living by a double standard? "Do what I say and not what I do" isn't a biblical way to live—especially with teenagers in our homes who are keenly alert to hypocrisy. As Henri Frederic Amiel observed, "The religion of a child depends upon what its mother and its father are, and not on what they say."[8]

> **"** Wherever you find yourself today, a new and dynamic family legacy is within reach, especially when you begin to teach the principles of discernment to those in your care.[7] **"**
>
> —**Robert G. DeMoss, Jr.**

No—we must be the first to pay the price by dealing radically with our own sinful habits, desires, and attitudes.

**Think about 1
Corinthians 11:1.**
Parents, is your life
such an example that
you could say this to
your teen?

We must ask the Holy Spirit to root out any worldliness in our hearts and make *us* blameless for the Father's glory. Not that we have to become perfect in order to teach our children discernment, but we definitely need to set the pace. A "do what I say *and* what I do" lifestyle is the only kind worth imitating.

The question is really a simple one: Are we as parents willing to do whatever it takes to obey God and lead our teens through these critical years? Are we prepared to...

> ❝ We as evangelical parents need to take a serious inventory of our own spiritual lives. Do we have a distinctly biblical worldview? Do we measure our behavior by the standards of Scripture or by the guy next door? Do our children hear us talk about God in a real and personal way, or do they perceive from our conversations that our faith is an impersonal subject to be studied? Are we living out our faith before them as authentic aliens or simply as tourists?
>
> We must ask ourselves other questions. Do our children see us spending time with God in prayer and Bible study or do they merely see us rushing from one religious activity to another? Have our children ever felt the liberty to ask us the tough questions about God's existence, the truth of Christianity, and the future of man? Do our children see us laboring to enlarge the kingdom of God, or seeking to enhance our own kingdoms? Do our children see us collecting 'things,' or investing in people?[9] ❞
>
> —Fran Sciacca

Get involved in their education by reviewing assignments, meeting with their teachers, and attending school functions?

Perhaps sacrifice for a private education or home schooling?

Spend time getting to know their friends so that they are less threatened when you share your concerns or offer advice?

Make your home a place where their friends feel accepted?

Develop and maintain standards about music, TV and movies, dress, and how they spend their time and money?

We don't have all the answers. Our children are going to be exposed to powerful influences at school and in the media. But we know the solution isn't to back off and hope they come through in the end. Remember Susan? That's what her parents did, and she ended up walking completely away from God and becoming the single mother of two children.

We're not trying to frighten you. It's just that we've seen too many young people raised in Christian homes by well-meaning parents who left their upbringing and God behind. Others are passively agreeable to church attendance. But they have no passion for Jesus Christ.

The biblical principle of sowing and reaping is true. If we pay the price, we can believe God for the results. If we teach our children to discern good from evil, God will deliver them from the powerful pull of the world. As we read in Proverbs 2:7, "He holds victory in store for the upright, he is a shield to those whose walk is blameless." What a tremendous promise! ■

QUESTIONS FOR PARENTS

1. Do you turn to others for parenting advice? (Dr. Spock doesn't count!) Why or why not?

2. Do you find yourself easily angered by your teen?

3. How would you answer a teen who said, "You learned from *your* mistakes—shouldn't I be free to make my own?"

4. Are you setting the pace in your household for discerning and overcoming sin in your life?

QUESTIONS FOR TEENS

1. Which would you prefer, pushover parents or parents with backbone?

2. Is there anything about your parents' training that you find especially difficult?

3. Who would you rather follow, peers or parents? Why?

4. Do you see "innocence" as a plus or a minus?

5. Is your conscience sharp or dull? How can you tell?

FACE TO FACE

1. "Wisdom and maturity aren't best gained by 'trial and error,'" say the authors (Page 60). Do you agree?

2. Discuss your answers to Question 3 on page 58.

3. How does one's relationship with parents affect one's relationship with God?

4. Parent(s), ask your teen to tell you if he or she feels you are being a hypocrite in any area of life. Listen humbly, and deal radically with any sin that is exposed!

Answer to Warm-Up
(from page 51): According to biologists, the answer is (D). When the population gets too big, lemmings take off in search of new nesting places. (Like the bottoms of lakes!) Could that explain why teens like to follow the crowd? (Source: *Grzimek's Animal Life Encyclopedia, Vol. II* (Kindler Verlag A.G. Zurich, 1968, pp. 326-28)

WANTED: IMPACT PLAYERS!

BIBLE STUDY   1 Timothy 4:12

WARM-UP   Imagine this: You're on safari in Africa, when suddenly you see a 4,000-pound rhino charging toward you. Your trusty guide offers you a choice of two rifles—one shoots two-ounce lead bullets, one shoots marshmallows.

What should you do?

A. Shoot the marshmallow gun

B. Shoot the regular gun

C. Climb the nearest tree

(See page 82 for answer)

PERSONAL STUDY   "It's just too hard."

"What do you mean?" we asked 15-year-old Lisa, who had approached us after a teaching session at a conference for teens.

"I mean, when I was younger I just accepted everything my parents said. I did as I was told. I talked to my friends about the Lord and invited them to our church a lot. But things have changed."

"In what way?"

"I don't know. I hear you talk about teens having a radical relationship with the Lord and I want that. I don't want to be just a follower. I *want* to influence my friends for good. I admire teens who don't care what everybody thinks of them because of their stand for Jesus Christ. But I just can't do it, Mr. and Mrs. Phillips. It's just too hard."

* * * * * *

Few teens enjoy hard work. Sweat. Hanging in there when the going gets tough. Picking themselves up time after time after time after falling or failing. Not getting first place. Trying out for the team if they're not convinced they'll make it. Going for an "A" when a "B" will do.

I (Benny) was an okay football player as a kid. Actually, I was pretty good. I started at age seven in the "ankle biter" league. As a wide receiver and eventually a quarterback, I accumulated quite a collection of trophies over the years. My boys' club coaches started grooming me to become the starting quarterback of my high school team. They were convinced I had the talent and the football "smarts" to do it.

But I ended up becoming the punter. Only the punter.

You see, I had gotten used to throwing or catching the touchdown passes. Receiving the congratulations. Not having to run laps because the coaches were working with me on my passing accuracy. Being the "star."

Think about Luke 9:23. What does God expect Christians to do every day? Is it easy or hard?

But my high school coach didn't know me from Adam. He actually expected me to *work* for the starting position! During those hot summer two-a-day practices, I had to run laps like everybody else. I wasn't the star. I was just another kid hoping to be the starting quarterback.

I didn't like having to prove myself, and it showed. My attitude cost me the position. The only time I touched the ball all season was right before I punted it. And after two minutes on the field I was back on the bench, waiting for the next punt.

We'll be honest with you. Living a pure and radical life as a teenager for Jesus Christ is hard work. Many teens want to make the team but they're not willing to pay the price. Like me, they end up sitting on the bench and watching others make the plays.

> **❝** 'The Christian ideal,' it is said, 'has not been tried and found wanting; it has been found difficult and left untried.'[1] **❞**
> —**G. K. Chesterton**

This reminds us of a message we once heard by pastor and author Bill Hybels. He talked about being "difference-makers" for Jesus Christ. As an example, he explained how athletic scouts and coaches try to recruit "impact players" for their teams. These are the men and women who make the plays. Inspire their teammates. Risk their bodies. Fight for the ball. Basically, whenever something is happening on the court or field, they seem to be in the middle of it.

God, too, is looking for "impact players," teenagers who are sold out to Jesus Christ. This kind of teen is willing to be misunderstood, criticized, or even rejected for obeying Christ. Dissatisfied with spectator Christianity, this difference-making teen is willing to pay the price to follow God's will for his or her life.

---

1 Whether you're an athlete or not, you know what it takes to be an "impact player" in a sport like football or basketball. What does it take to be an "impact player" for Christ? (List two or three things in the space below.)

A Reason Behind The Rules

During the teen years, young people begin coming to grips with things they never questioned in their childhood. They have a legitimate need to understand the "whys" of life.

"Why is commitment to a church important?"

"Why do some teens drift from God?"

"Why is it important to choose my friends carefully?"

"Why can it be harmful to spend extended time alone with someone of the opposite sex?"

"Why am I not allowed to do some of the things my friends do?"

Parents can feel threatened when their teens start asking "why." Fearing that this is the first sign of rebellion, our knee-jerk response may be to answer, "Because that's the way it is," or "Because I said so."

Yes, many teens ask these kinds of questions because they are challenging their parents' authority and leadership. In such cases, Dad and Mom should firmly and consistently address this attitude. However, some teens are simply looking for answers that will give them greater understanding of what's *behind* the standards they've been taught. They don't necessarily want to disobey their parents' rules; they just want to understand why they *should* obey.

Think about Ephesians 6:4. Are parents disobeying God when they refuse to answer legitimate questions from their teens?

69

In other words, they are looking for convictions. And until they learn to develop firm convictions from God's unchanging Word, they will never be impact players for Jesus Christ.

What Do You Do When Nobody Is Watching?

Most dictionaries define the word "conviction" similarly to Funk & Wagnalls: "a firm belief." It is something you are convinced of or feel strongly about. It's a "nobody can change my mind on this" mentality.

Now don't get me wrong. I'm not talking about a cocky, "in your face" attitude about minor things like who's the best player in the NBA or whether schools should have dress codes. Biblical convictions aren't based on opinions or personal preferences or what everybody around you thinks. They are based on the values and principles taught in Scripture. If you have a *conviction* about something you believe in it *firmly*. Even when it's unpopular. And not only because your parents or youth leader say you should believe it—or because they're watching.

Let me give you an example.

From boyhood, Mike was taught to respect and obey his parents' authority. He obeyed because it was expected of him (and he knew there would be consequences if he didn't!). As he approached the teen years he would sometimes question his parents' authority in his own mind. At times he felt they were too strict or their decisions seemed unreasonable.

Mike and his parents worked hard on their relationship, especially during those early teen years. When he had questions, he knew he could talk to his parents. And he knew to ask respectfully:

"Dad, I'm not trying to change your mind or anything, but would you mind explaining *why* I can't drive to the game?" rather than "I can't drive? Why? You're treating me like a little kid again!"

Digging deeper:
Queen Esther's appeal to King Xerxes is a classic example of how one can respectfully question a decision made by someone in authority. You'll find the story in the book of Esther, chapters 4-8.

One day at school several of Mike's classmates got on the subject of parents. They were complaining that their parents didn't seem to trust them.

"Hey, I'm almost an adult," said Joe. "I don't think my parents should be in charge of things like when I can use the car or how long I should talk on the phone." The others nodded in agreement.

Mike had noticed this kind of critical attitude toward parents before. Now he knew it was time to speak up.

"Listen, guys. We don't always have to agree with our parents but we're supposed to respect and obey them."

"But I'm eighteen years old!" Joe protested.

"I know," Mike continued. "All I'm saying is that our parents are given their authority by God. If they make mistakes, that's between them and him. Bottom line, unless they ask us to do something wrong, the Bible just tells us to obey. Besides, sometimes I think there are good reasons why we teenagers can't be trusted."

Silence. A few of the kids probably rolled their eyes or exchanged glances that said "this guy is really weird."

> 66 Never be ashamed of letting men see that you want to go to heaven. Think it no disgrace to show yourself to be a servant of God. Never be afraid of doing what is right.[3] 99
>
> —J.C. Ryle

But Mike wasn't surprised. He knew that speaking up wouldn't make him the next candidate for class president.

This incident shows how important convictions are. As a toddler, Mike may have responded to his parents' authority because they were bigger or louder than he was. Or because he learned that disobedience resulted in discipline. As a teen, Mike is now obviously *convinced in his heart* of the value of parental authority. He has wrestled through this issue. He has his own "firm belief" about it.

His parents weren't watching. His youth leader wasn't listening. As far as his reputation with the guys went, he had nothing to gain and everything to lose by stating his convictions. That takes guts, especially among your peers.

We know Mike. He's not a "wind me up and I'll obey my parents" robot. He struggles at times over his parents' decisions. He admits he doesn't always agree with them. He has wondered at times if they were being overly protective of him. And, as we said earlier, he respectfully appeals when he doesn't understand or agree.

But when the rubber meets the road and they say "no," he chooses to obey. No longer because he's trying to avoid punishment or because he has exhausted his ability to

Think about Proverbs 10:17. How does *your* response to your parents' discipline affect the influence you have on your peers?

manipulate them. He has simply chosen to believe the truth of Scripture: "Children, obey your parents in the Lord, for this is right. 'Honor your father and mother'—which is the first commandment with a promise—'that it may go well with you and that you may enjoy long life on the earth'" (Ephesians 6:1-3).

---

2 Jenny's classmates laugh at her because she doesn't wear miniskirts. Listed below are some possible responses. Put a "C" in the box beside the ones you think reflect genuine conviction.

❏ "Mom won't let me buy the skirts I like."

❏ "I only wear these to hide my heavy thighs."

❏ "I'd rather look like my mother than Madonna."

❏ "My parents are trying to turn me into a nun!"

❏ "I really don't like having boys look at my legs."

Firm, biblical beliefs are the backbone of a solid Christian life. Young men and women who have strong convictions:

Recognize that sin is more than just an occasional temptation. It's something we do instinctively apart from God (see Romans 3:10, 23). Teens need firm beliefs to resist the pull toward worldliness. Only strong convictions will make you able to say "no" to sin and compromise.

Are better prepared to face temptation. Adolescence involves some unique challenges—peer pressure being one of the biggest. The teen who isn't prepared will almost certainly fail the test. But those who have well-developed convictions (parents, your help is critical) won't be caught off guard when temptation strikes. "Peer pressure has no power in and of itself," writes Dr. David Elkind. "The peer group is powerful only because there are teenagers...who lack the inner strengths that would weigh against conforming."[4] Strength of conviction can overcome the strength of temptation.

Provide a godly example for their peers (see 1 Timothy 4:12). Teens, your peers are looking for people to follow. That's why most of them are unwilling to stand out or be different. I'm not suggesting you be "different" just to prove you're a Christian. Teens with convictions stand out for their *character* and ability to *withstand peer pressure*,

Think about Acts 17:5-7. Wouldn't you like to have the kind of reputation Paul and his friends had?

not because they dress, act, or talk weird. "Difference-makers" have strong convictions that command respect and set them apart for God in a generation of fit-in-with-the-crowd-at-all-costs conformers.

Five Critical Convictions

Every parent and teen should discuss the specific areas in which convictions are needed. For your consideration, here is the list we use with our teens.

Respect for authority. As they approach adulthood, teens are often tempted to assert themselves prematurely. Make their own decisions. Distance themselves from those in authority. Question the rightness or wrongness of a decision made for them. And complain about how Dad or the coach or the teacher is out of touch.

Mike and his parents are great role models for us all. The wise parent will allow his or her teen to ask questions respectfully or express confusion about why a decision was made. As they talk back and forth, they will understand the issue and each other better. This open and honest dialogue is important to the parent-teen relationship.

But equally, if not more, important is the teen's need to develop the inner humility to see *God's* authority in his or her life *expressed though those in God-ordained positions of authority.* The maturing teen chooses to believe the truth of Romans 13:1-2: "...for there is no authority except that which God has established...Consequently, he who rebels against the authority is rebelling against what God has instituted, and those who do so will bring judgment on themselves."

> ❝ The youth world is especially effective in enforcing conformity. Its fundamental law is 'Never side with an authority against another youth'...There is no greater offense in the youth world.[5] ❞
> **—Michael Keating**

Like Mike, teens need to become convinced in their hearts of this biblical truth. By developing a firm conviction about respecting those in authority—especially their own parents—they set themselves up to enjoy God's grace and blessing throughout the critical adolescent years.

Appearance. It's not hard for a parent to tell when adolescence has arrived. Last year you had to remind your child to take a shower. Brush his teeth. Comb her hair. Wear matching clothes. Find a pair of shoes...and put them on the right feet.

Digging deeper: What is God impressed by when he looks at a person? Even the great prophet Samuel was fooled by this one! (See 1 Samuel 16:1-7)

Now it seems your teen's favorite spot in the house is in front of the bathroom mirror. Drying and spraying and moussing and combing his hair. Trying on one pair of earrings after another. Agonizing over pimples. Applying make-up and perfume or cologne—*lots* of it! Making sure her blouse is tucked in (but not too much...the "baggy" look is back).

Teens, let's be real: How much of what you wear is determined by what everyone else is wearing? Will those basketball shoes with the special air pockets or pumps really help your game...or just impress your teammates? Do you want that new hairstyle because it's *your* preference and will look nice on you? Or because "everybody's wearing it this way"? Are you especially looking forward to the youth meeting tonight because you hope to hear from God? Or is it because you're going to wear that new outfit you just bought with birthday money? Are you willing to compromise modesty for the sake of attention from the opposite sex?

These are hard questions. Only discerning, courageous teens will deal honestly with them. Parents, we need to help our teens get in touch with their real motives. And we need to admit and overcome any misguided motives of our *own* that drive us to want our teen to be the best-dressed or most popular in the crowd.

Having a *conviction* about your appearance means that, if asked, you would say something like this: "The decisions I make about my clothes, hair, or fashion are between me and my parents. It's not wrong to want to be attractive. But I won't allow my choices to be determined by what's 'in' or what's acceptable to my peers. And I won't compromise biblical principles like modesty, femininity (for girls), or dignity (for guys) just to get attention from others."

---

3 Parents, let's see how well you know the world of youth fashion:

■ What is the current "look"?

■ What designers/labels are most popular?

■ What style was "in" when you were a teen?

Entertainment and leisure. Today's teens are the "media generation." Never before in history have young people been exposed to so many fast-paced, visually stimulating, entertainment-oriented influences.

We don't need to say much about the power the media can hold. We've all heard of people who imitated violent crimes they saw in a movie, or teens who committed suicide after hearing about it in a song. And, as parents, we remember saying, "But I don't really listen to the words. I just like the music." (It's funny that 20 years later we can *still* remember those words we "weren't listening to" from that old '60s song!)

Think about Proverbs 4:23. How can you "guard your heart" from the media's powerful influence?

Teens, we know what some of you are thinking. You don't listen to or watch "the really bad stuff." You've never attempted suicide or murdered anyone after watching a movie or listening to the radio. You're not one of those mindless youths who are easily influenced by things. Why all the fuss about a little background music or some video rentals?

Trust us on this one. What you see and hear leaves its mark on your heart and mind.

We're not suggesting that all TV is bad, all secular music is sinful, and all movies will hurt your walk with God. But we *are* saying many teens underestimate the media's influence. For the most part, the entertainment industry is promoting behavior and attitudes that grieve God. Don't think you can be exposed to it year after year and not be affected. That would be as stupid as smoking two packs of cigarettes a day and thinking it didn't increase your chance of getting cancer.

> ❝ Have you ever spent an evening or a Saturday with your eyes glued to the television? You should do a dozen things, but you keep gawking at the inane objects wiggling before you. Afterwards, you sense an empty feeling in your stomach knowing you have spent four or five utterly wasted hours and you will never again have those hours back to use.[6] ❞
>
> —Jerry White

When it comes to television, movies, music, or any other form of entertainment, ask yourself, "Is this going to increase or decrease my appetite for God?"

Does that seem like an unusual question? We ask it because teens have a strong desire for entertainment. An "appetite" for sights and sounds—especially *loud* sounds! You enjoy things that stir and excite you. And with the entertainment industry investing billions of dollars to satisfy this craving for stimulation, you can have it all with a flick of the remote control.

The long-term consequences reach far beyond what we may think. Over time, today's entertained teen can easily get bored with the things of God. Sunday-morning worship is pretty tame compared to what a lot of kids hear during the week, isn't it? (Even in churches with good worship bands!) Teens who make their selections from the world's menu lose their appetite for the kingdom of God.

When you gobble up junk food, you're not hungry for dinner.

Digging deeper:
Young men and women who are hungry for God will turn their eyes toward him and away from evil (Psalm 101:2-4, 119:37).

Is your relationship with God weak? Are you bored with worship? Are your Christian friendships superficial? Is your devotional life inconsistent (or non-existent)? Do you find yourself wanting to watch movies or listen to music you know God would give two thumbs down? Then you're probably eating too much "junk." And junk is sometimes a lot tastier than the good, nutritious stuff.

If you're careful about what goes *in* your heart and mind, you won't struggle so much with what comes *out*. Parents and teens, God wants our diet to be full of the "good stuff"—even when it's less appealing to our flesh than a lot of other things. Having biblical convictions about entertainment will make us a lot hungrier for God.

Involvement in the church. For some well-meaning Christians, church is one of many activities in a given week. There's school. Piano lessons. Soccer practice. An orthodontist appointment. And church.

For a couple of hours a week, they make church a priority. Perhaps they also take part in a youth group meeting or outing, or even an overnighter with a Christian friend. But for many teens, church is about as exciting as reading the dictionary. Sure, it's a good thing to have around, and it often comes in handy. But who enjoys sitting down to read the *dictionary*?

Judging by the lives of most American teens, the exciting, important things happen every day *but* Sunday. "It seems obvious," writes Dr. Robert Laurent, "that the gospel of Jesus Christ is making little difference in the lives of many teenagers."[7]

Why does it seem obvious? Because attendance at church meetings is sometimes the *only* sign that a teenager has any interest in God. This was certainly true of me (Benny) as a teen. I showed up on Sunday mornings—but my friends knew I only "went to church" because my parents required it. Any other time I dressed and talked and acted just like my non-Christian peers.

We have the privilege of interacting with a lot of teenagers who are *not* all your typical, "I go to church because my parents make me" teens. Many actually enjoy the church. They have good friends in the church. Their parents may be leaders in the church. Quite a few serve in children's ministry, help with tape duplication, or sing in the worship group.

But only a handful have a *conviction* about their involvement in the church.

When people hear the word "church," most think of a building with a steeple and stained glass. Yet to say, "I'm going to church" is to misrepresent what the Bible says about the church. The church is the people of God, those who have been called out of the world and into his kingdom. As one man has described it, the church isn't an organization—it's an organism. It's alive! It's not made with brick and steel. The church is made of people.

And the church is absolutely vital for your maturity in Christ.

To grow in God, you need a church family who will encourage you. Teach and train you. Motivate you. Let you know you're not the only one who struggles in various areas. Show you how to overcome temptation and sin. And, yes, lovingly correct you when you're being selfish or proud or disrespectful.

---

4 In your opinion, which of these statements describe the church accurately? (Check all that apply.)

❏ A place to nap on Sunday mornings

❏ A brick building with stained glass windows

❏ A group of people growing together in God

❏ A place to hang out with friends

❏ A source of training and discipleship

❏ A boring place where people make you feel guilty

❏ An exciting place where God reveals himself

Think about Ephesians 4:16. What part has God given you to play in your church?

Teens with a biblical conviction about the church recognize their tendency to be independent. They know how easy it is to think they're doing okay spiritually when they're really not. Though they want to grow in the Lord, they are very aware of the pressure to be accepted by their peers and to find their identity among friends or at school. So how can you resist those urges? By first acknowledging your dependence on Jesus Christ. And then recognizing your need for God's people, the church. Don't fool yourself into thinking you can make it on your own. Choose to identify with the people of God.

You can give your life to a lot of activities and things. Academics. Sports. School clubs. Music. Becoming the "best dressed" or the "most likely to succeed." Things that may bring you attention and recognition from your peers. And things that aren't necessarily wrong or sinful.

Or you can give these critical years of your life to something eternal. Growing in Christ-like character. Serving others. Learning from those who are wiser and more experienced. Building relationships, not just with your peers, but with your parents and other adults. Standing up in your generation for what is right. Saying "no" to temptation and compromise and worldliness.

Don't try to do it alone. You can't. (Neither can we.) You need the church—the people of God. And you know what that means? Getting up early on Sundays even when you're tired. Reaching out to the younger teens when you'd rather be with your own friends. Greeting new kids in the youth group. Showing respect and honor to your leaders. Humbly admitting your need for help and discipleship. Viewing friendships with Christians and attendance at meetings not as just another "chore," but as *the* way for you to grow in Jesus Christ and discover his plan for your life.

Involvement in the church isn't optional. It's standard equipment!

And parents, it begins with us! We can't expect our teens to value the church if we don't. We can't give our "leftover" time and money and energy to the church and then agonize over our children's lack of spiritual zeal. Attending meetings isn't enough—especially for teens. They want something to *believe* in…to get excited about …to build their lives on. They want to *see* Christianity, not just hear about it.

Will they channel their passion into the church—or the world?

Speech. What?! Okay, you're beginning to get the idea about convictions. They're things we feel strongly about, things we stand up for even when it's unpopular.

> **❝** One cannot claim to be a Christian and at the same time claim to be outside the church. To do so is at the least hypocrisy —at the worst, blasphemy.[8] **❞**
>
> —**Charles Colson**

Think about Mark 12:30. Is this how you love God and the church?

So why the need for a *conviction* about *talking*?

Because many teens don't seem to know what the Bible says about speech. They laugh at off-color jokes. Have "private" talks with friends and then leak the details to others. If you'll listen closely, you'll notice a lot of their conversations start with, "Did you hear about what so-and-so did?" or "Can you believe what so-and-so said?"

Because most teens talk a lot—on the phone, at school, in the halls before the youth meeting, on the phone afterwards—the truth of Proverbs 10:19 is soon apparent: "When words are many, sin is not absent."

Our home-schooled son Josh and his friend, Andy, recently began taking two classes at a small Christian high school. By the end of their second day, most of the school (especially the girls, it seemed) knew a whole lot about these guys. They play basketball (great—the team needs some help!). They've been home-schooled all their lives (how boring!). One is a pastor's son (*he's* probably no fun). And, most incredible of all, THEY DON'T DATE!!!

Josh was really surprised. He'd been there for less than four hours over two days and his reputation in some significant areas had already been established. By day three, he was fielding questions about dating and schooling several times a day. In the halls, rest rooms, and over lunch, the word spread from one to another.

"You're not gonna believe what I heard about…"

"Have you seen the new guys? Did you hear they…?"

"I saw you talking to them. Did you ask about…?"

Teens are curious. They want to be "in the know" about others. And they are often tempted to put others down in order to feel better about themselves.

The Bible calls it gossip.

---

5 In the past week, have you said—or listened to—something about someone that might have hurt his/her reputation?

Briefly give the details.

How can you make things right again?

Digging deeper: Here are a few biblical passages to help you develop a conviction about gossip: Psalm 101:5; Proverbs 11:13, 17:9, 18:8, 20:19; James 3:7-8; and 1 Peter 3:10.

From our years of observing and leading teens, we have come to believe gossip is the biggest reason why teen friendships and church youth groups fail. Why? Because gossip is as dangerous as throwing a lit match into a gas tank. It blows friendships apart. People's feelings are hurt. The Holy Spirit is grieved. Teens begin to focus more on what somebody did or didn't do than on who they are on the inside. The youth group becomes polarized into "cliques" who act and dress and feel the same.

The Bible talks specifically about the damage gossip can do to us and others. It also provides a standard for godly communication:

> Do not let any unwholesome [critical, judgmental, suspicious, embarrassing to others] talk come out of your mouths [this includes listening to it come out of other's mouths, too], but only what is helpful for building others up [encouraging, uplifting, honoring them]..." (Ephesians 4:29, additions ours).

This verse alone rules out many teen (and adult!) conversations. If we feel we have something negative or confrontational to say about someone, we are instructed by God to speak to him or her privately (see Matthew 18:15). In all other cases, we should discuss other people only in a positive or encouraging way.

> ❝ Never listen to accounts of the frailties of others; and if anyone should complain to you of another, humbly ask him not to speak of him at all.[9] ❞
> —**John of the Cross**

This means no talking about that "interesting" outfit Sheila wore to the meeting. Who David likes now. Why Jim has been acting a little funny lately. Whether Susan realizes how loud she talks. Or the "normally I wouldn't bring this up but we really need to pray for so-and-so" excuse for talking about someone's struggles or unattractive habits. You'll never be able to tame your tongue, teens—and the same is true for parents—until you develop a deep-seated conviction about what God wants to come out of your mouths. (Getting God's perspective on gossip is so important that we'll dig into it more deeply in Study Eight.)

* * * * * *

There are plenty of other areas which call for biblical conviction, including many of the issues addressed in this book. But these five will give you a headstart as you work toward being God-dependent rather than peer-dependent.

Standing alone isn't easy. It will take courage to communicate your convictions. And it may cost you some friends who prefer to "blend in" with the crowd. But at least you won't waste your teen years on the bench. You'll be honoring God. You'll be storing up eternal rewards. You'll be making a difference for Christ and his kingdom. You'll be an "impact player." ■

QUESTIONS FOR PARENTS

1. Do you have *small*, *moderate*, or *big* ambitions for your teen's future? What are they?

2. Are you a "difference maker" among *your* peers?

3. Do you exercise your authority in a way that encourages your teen to respect you?

4. How does your appetite for entertainment compare with your appetite for God?

5. Does your life demonstrate wholehearted commitment to the Lord and the church?

QUESTIONS FOR TEENS

1. What is one thing you do simply because your parents tell you to?

2. What is one thing you do because you're convinced in your heart that it's right?

3. When you're with others your age, do you stand out or blend in with the crowd?

4. If someone started gossiping to you about someone else, how could you respond?

5. Are you willing to *work* to be an impact player for Jesus?

FACE TO FACE

1. "Strength of conviction can overcome the strength of temptation" (Page 72). Discuss ways in which this is true for you.

2. On a scale of one to five, rate each other as follows:
Teen: Attitude when questioning parents' decisions
Parent: Attitude when responding to teen's questions

3. In addition to the five areas listed in this study (Pages 73-80), where do you see a need for biblical convictions?

4. Why do we place so much emphasis on appearance?

5. Is your current church involvement causing you to grow in Christ? How? If not, what needs to change?

RECOMMENDED READING

J.C. Ryle, *Thoughts For Young Men* (Taken from 1886 edition by Wm. Hunt & Co., London. Revised edition ©1993 published by Calvary Press, P.O. Box 805, Amityville, NY 11701, (800) 789-8175.)

Elisabeth Elliot, *Let Me Be A Woman: Notes To My Daughter on the Meaning of Womanhood* (Wheaton, IL: Tyndale House Publishers, Inc., 1976)

Answer to Warm-Up
(from page 67): Your goal, of course, is to make such an impact on the rhino that he doesn't make an impact on you! If you're a good shot and the rhino is far enough away, the two-ounce bullet should do the trick (Answer B). If you're not a good shot and the nearby tree is at least 12 inches in diameter, you may want to get vertical (Answer C). The marshmallow gun is probably not the best choice, unless the rhino likes eating marshmallows more than he likes trampling hunters (Answer A).

WHATCHA DOIN' FRIDAY NIGHT?

BIBLE STUDY 1 Timothy 5:1-2

WARM-UP Assuming the statistics are correct, Friday nights are *violent* nights for many teenage couples. Researchers at California State University in Sacramento surveyed 256 young couples who were age 17 and 18. Can you guess how many reported violence or threats of violence in their relationship?

A. 7%

B. 19%

C. 28%

D. 35%

E. 44%

(See page 97 for answer)

PERSONAL STUDY You're walking down the hall of the church building on Sunday morning and notice Todd. He glances up and smiles. In fact, he starts walking toward you! You're glad you remembered to brush your teeth that morning and hope your hair barrette is still in place.

"Hi, Sarah," he says, warmly. After returning his greeting you chat for a few minutes…then he pops the question.

"So, are going to the ice skating party Friday night?"

"Yes—but I probably won't skate. After we went last winter, I was sore for days from falling on the ice!"

"Well, how 'bout if you had some help?" he asks. "I do okay. And I was thinking maybe I could pick you up early to go out for a burger first."

"Sure, Todd. That would be great!"

You can't believe it…the coolest guy in the youth group just asked you out! And he drives a great car! Wait till the rest of the girls hear about this. As the Sunday meeting starts, you are already mentally scanning your closet to figure out what you will wear....

* * * * * *

Dating is probably the favorite pastime among American teens. As parents, we remember going with our dates to football games...movies...bowling alleys...parties... amusement parks. Now that we have teens, we want them to enjoy wholesome, memorable times with their friends. Times they will look back on fondly for years to come.

As teens, you have a growing desire to relate to the opposite sex. A few years ago you were content to hang out with just the guys or the girls. In fact, you preferred it that way. But not any more. These days, activities and events are a lot more fun when you share them with mixed company, right?

Think about Proverbs 14:12. Just because something looks right or feels right doesn't mean it *is* right!

For many Christian teens, this growing interest in the opposite sex leads to dating. Youth group and school activities help you get to know different people. Soon, you may feel attracted to one of them. You talk. You look forward to seeing one another. You exchange phone numbers. You think of one another and begin talking about each other to your friends. When you're together it's as if no one else is in the room. And people begin to think of you as a "couple." Cool.

You assume the best way to deepen your friendship is to spend some undistracted time together. You know—to be able to talk without your little sister listening or butting in. To walk through the mall holding hands. No *worldly* behavior like you see going on between some of the kids in school—things you would never do as a Christian. Just time to get to know one another and the freedom to express some affection.

In other words, it's time for a date.

---

1 Pretend you're back at age nine or ten. Which of the following were you worried about getting if a boy or girl touched you? (Check all that apply)

❑ Chicken pox   ❑ The plague   ❑ Warts

❑ Pneumonia   ❑ Cooties   ❑ Cancer

❑ Leprosy   ❑ Measles   ❑ All of these

84

What Your Great-Great Grandparents Never Did

You may be surprised to know that dating is a recent event in American history. Before the "date," teens got to know each other through church or community activities. They served together in the neighborhood. The girls helped prepare food for guys who were helping build a neighbor's house or barn. Sometimes they were introduced when a girl's dad hired a young man to help harvest the crops. Or they met at a community square dance or church picnic.

As the friendship developed into something more, it remained closely tied to the family, community, and church. Young people had very little time alone without friends or adults around. There was no car for driving around on Friday night. No telephone for long talks after school. No movie theaters or roller skating rinks where teens could hold hands. Couples would be allowed to talk alone in the parlor, but parents were never far away. If a young man and woman thought their friendship was headed toward marriage, and if their parents agreed, they committed themselves to a formal relationship known as "courtship."

> **"** When it comes to relationships in America, teenagers are in a frenzy. Like crazed sharks, teens are in a state of confusion, grasping at anything that promises fulfillment or happiness.[1] **"**
>
> **—Joshua Harris**

Back then, couples didn't make a big deal of being romantically attracted to each other. In fact, as Ellen Rothman points out in her book *Hearts and Hands: A History of Courtship in America*, people were suspicious of such feelings:

> Romance required caution: it was fertile soil for a flower that could all too easily overrun the garden. Both women and men used *romantic* to describe feelings that were childish, uncontrolled, and unreliable...*Romantic* connoted a lack not merely of seriousness but of maturity. One had to be careful that romantic diversions did not interfere with one's adult responsibilities.[2]

However, as cities spread and grew in the late 1800s, things began to change. More and more young women began attending high school and college. Both young men and women were working in shops, factories, and classrooms. The home, church, and community were no longer

New England pastor Jonathan Edwards, best known for his part in America's "Great Awakening," had strong, biblical convictions about dating. Listen to the way his biographer described him:

[Jonathan Edwards] was a great enemy to young people's unseasonable company-keeping and frolicking, as he looked upon it as a great means of corrupting and ruining youth. And he thought the excuse many parents make for tolerating their children in it (viz. that it is the custom, and others' children practice it, which renders it difficult, and even impossible to restrain theirs) was insufficient and frivolous; and manifested a great degree of stupidity, on supposition the practice was hurtful and pernicious to their souls. And when some of his children grew up he found no difficulty in restraining them from this pernicious practice; but they cheerfully complied with the will of their parents herein. He allowed not his children to be from home after nine o'clock at night, when they went abroad to see their friends and companions. Neither were they allowed to sit up much after that time, in his own house, when any came to make them a visit. If any gentleman desired acquaintance with his daughters; after handsomely introducing himself, by properly consulting the parents, he was allowed all proper opportunity for it; a room and fire, if needed: but must not intrude on the proper hours of rest and sleep, or the religion and order of the family.[3]

—Samuel Hopkins

the hub of social life. Teens met at school or work, and parents were less and less involved in their children's relationships.

This is when dating really began. It was called "going somewhere." Couples would take the train or streetcar to some show or a dance miles away from home. When bicycles became popular in the 1890s couples discovered a new way to spend time alone together.

By the 1930s things had really changed. Cars and movie theaters were the rage. Courtship had pretty much been replaced by dating. People bounced from dating partner to dating partner with little sense of commitment. And the standards for how couples acted had relaxed dramatically. Without Mom or Uncle Henry or the pastor around, there was certainly a lot more "freedom."

In earlier years young Billy and Susie spent limited time together, almost always with supervision. Now they could hop in a car together; go to a movie followed by dancing; and return home in the middle of the night having spent hours and hours alone. It doesn't take a brain surgeon to figure out some of the negative effects of the changes that were taking place in society.

By the 1950s "going steady" was common practice among American high schoolers. Billy and Susie now spent regular time alone together and dated only one another. Being emotionally and physically affectionate with one another was okay because they were "going

Digging deeper: Do you think a young man and woman alone know what it takes to build a successful relationship? (See Proverbs 11:14, 15:22, 20:18, and 24:6)

together." That is, until Susie lost interest in Billy and started "going with" someone else.[4]

Thanks for your patience with all this. And there's a good reason for this quick history lesson on dating. It's important for you to know that dating isn't the way to build a successful relationship with the opposite sex. In fact, it's proving to be a failure! Dating came about as young people distanced themselves from their families, churches, and communities. When couples left the safety of others, they began to relate in ways that would have shocked teens a few generations ago.

Bottom line: Dating wasn't God's idea.

More and more parents and teens are realizing that dating isn't all it's cracked up to be. It can be harmful to all teens, but especially to those who really want to live radical lives for Jesus Christ.

Why? Let's find out.

The Dangers Of Dating

Some of you were doing fine until you got to this part of the book. Maybe what you've read so far is different than stuff you've heard before, but you could see the wisdom of it.

Now you're wondering if we've gone over the edge.

"No dating? Even if it's another Christian? Even when Mom thinks she's great? How in the world are we going to get to know people of the opposite sex without dating? And someday I'd like to get married—explain *that* one to me!"

> **❝** The American institution of dating is not improving the church or the family.[5] **❞**
>
> **—Jim West**

Relax. We'll discuss the how-do-I-get-to-know-people issues later. For now, let us be honest with you about the harm dating can cause.

As a Christian, you must live your life according to what the Bible says. Right? Not what others are doing or what society says is okay. Remember the truth of Romans 12:2: Don't let the world squeeze you into its mold. You're called to be different!

Think about Psalm 119:9. How can a young person be assured of living a pure life?

Now the Bible never says, "Thou shalt not date." You won't find that among the Ten Commandments or anywhere else. Why? Because it was never even a question! In biblical times, before there were malls and movie theaters and McDonalds, young men and women felt no need to "experiment" with romance. When they were ready for

87

marriage, they (or their parents) picked a partner and started a home. It was simple. That's why the Bible doesn't say *anything* about dating. It describes only three kinds of relationships between men and women: friendship, engagement (also called betrothal), and marriage. (You don't read about Isaac or Esther or David "dating around" until they decided who they would marry.)

---

2 Before you read any further, complete the following sentence in your own words: *I think dating is good/bad (pick one) for teens because...*

Because the Bible doesn't specifically say "no dating," some might think it's okay. After all, we're living in different times, right? But if you really want to live a sold-out life for God and let *him* have control of your life, you won't just look for the "thou shalt nots." Instead, you'll look for the *principles* about how to live. And in addition to its many teachings about purity, we believe God's Word shows guys and girls a much better way to relate.

As a young man, Timothy received much advice from the apostle Paul. On one occasion, Paul specifically told Timothy how to act toward the young ladies in his church: "treat...younger women as sisters, with absolute purity" (1 Timothy 5:1, 2). No doubt this advice was meant to safeguard Timothy in his role as a church leader. But we believe this principle applies equally well to today's teens.

Think about this for a minute. In fact, we'd like to ask you a few questions. You first, guys. Would you...

Walk through the mall holding your sister's hand?

Hurry to class so you could sit by your sister?

Check out your sister's outfit and pay her special compliments?

Digging deeper: Read
1 Thessalonians 4:3-7.
Do you think teens
"take advantage" of
each other (see vs. 6)
when they flirt or relate
in selfish ways?

Before you hurt yourself laughing, girls, let's throw a few questions your way: Do you...

Wear your hair the way your brother likes it?

Daydream about seeing your brother at the youth meeting?

Talk to your friends about how cute your brother is?

If we apply Paul's teaching not just to leaders but to unmarried people in general, then the Bible's teaching seems pretty clear. Until God shows who you'll marry, teens, you're to treat those of the opposite sex as you would your own brothers and sisters.

(For some of you, this may be hard to swallow because you treat your brothers and sisters pretty badly. God wants *you* to begin by learning how to love them...be kind to them...serve them. Start there for now!)

With this principle in place, let's look now at ten of the most common problems with dating.

Selfishness. Dating relationships are usually built on me-centered thinking like this: "As long as I like you and you don't do anything to embarrass or bug me, we'll date." When you no longer enjoy being with the person, you simply dump him or her for the next dating partner. (Unless you're the one being dumped.)

> **❝** God calls us to relationships in which we seek more to bless than to be blessed, more to give than to receive. God calls us to relationships in which honesty and integrity reign supreme. Brothers and sisters pursue these goals with abandon. Whatever will increase the blessing for their brothers and sisters, brothers and sisters pursue it.[6] **❞**
>
> —John Holzmann

Jealousy and possessiveness. Anyone who shows the "wrong" kind of attention to someone you're dating better watch out! Whether you say it or not, what you're thinking is, "He or she is mine. Back off!"

Flirting. Flirting isn't just an "innocent" way of relating as teens. In fact, we believe it's sin. Simply put, flirting is acting or dressing in such a way as to entice someone of the opposite sex. Those who flirt selfishly flaunt their external assets (like an attractive figure or outgoing personality) in order to draw attention to themselves. To flirt with someone is to say, "I'm available and interested in a romantic relationship with you." Sound a little dramatic? Not if you're honest. And though it may seem harmless, it's not. It can hurt you—the attention your flirting brings can easily get out of control. It also hurts others by stirring up romantic desires which the Bible teaches should be reserved for marriage.

Have you flirted with your brother or sister recently? We didn't think so. And we recommend you take that same approach with others.

Digging deeper: How does the Bible describe a truly beautiful woman? (See 1 Peter 3:3-5)

Too much emphasis on externals. Dating creates a very artificial environment among teens. The emphasis is on how you look, dress, and smell. Even the smallest details of jewelry, type of shoes, or clothing labels take on great significance in order to "get" a certain guy or girl. Inward character often becomes a non-issue.

Emotional pain. Your parents probably remember the song, "Breaking Up is Hard to Do." And it is. Countless teens today—including teens who regularly go to church— have had their hearts broken by a former boyfriend or girlfriend. The pain of this rejection can create deep and lasting problems like distrust, fear of commitment, and bitterness.

In over twenty years of pastoral ministry, we have counseled many couples with serious marital problems. Most were suffering from these and other consequences of heartbreaking teen romances. Don't let it happen to you!

> **❝** The vast majority of parents want their children to abstain from sexual relationships until marriage. However, we have failed to see that abstinence should include emotional abstinence as well. In other words, if we permit our children to develop boyfriend-girlfriend relationships before they are ready to get married, we are simply asking for sexual temptation, and in many cases, sexual trouble.[7] **❞**
>
> —**Michael Farris**

"Divorce" mentality. Did you know the divorce rate in America began to soar after dating began? That's no mere coincidence.

It is our firm belief that dating teaches young people to bail out of relationships when they are no longer enjoyable. They then take this skill at "breaking up" with them to the altar. What happens if the marriage stops being "fun"? They throw their spouse away just as they have numerous girlfriends or boyfriends in the past. Dating becomes a "trial marriage" where many people act married without the level of commitment God requires. (Yes, many teens carry out this "trial marriage" relationship at very early ages!)

Isolation. In the days when courtship was the formal stage between friendship and marriage, parents were expected to be closely involved in a developing relationship. The goal of today's date, though, is for the couple to get alone—often to say and do things they wouldn't say or do around others. Joshua Harris comments, "Dating separates two people from the protection of those who love them the most [their parents] and sets them up to fail."[8] Is he just another middle-aged grump? No—Joshua is 18!

Dating prevents young people from seeing each other as they really are. And by isolating them from their peers, it robs them of the opportunity to build true friendships that stand the tests of disappointment, misunderstanding, and conflict.

Ask yourself this question: How do you best get to know someone? When you're alone and they're acting their best to impress you? Or when you can see them in group situations, interacting with others?

---

3 Listed below are the qualities of true love described in 1 Corinthians 13:4-8. In your opinion, which of these are *not* typically true of teen dating relationships?

❑ Patient

❑ Kind

❑ Not envious

❑ Humble

❑ Polite

❑ Committed to truth

❑ Not selfish

❑ Not easily angered

❑ Forgiving

❑ Protective

❑ Trustful

❑ Hopeful

❑ Persevering

❑ Unfailing

Temptation and compromise. Dating exposes teens to frequent temptation. The emotional and physical attraction that sparks the desire to date someone also produces other desires. We know of many churchgoing teens who have been spiritually shipwrecked because they made wrong choices with a dating partner.

Negative comparisons and poor self-image. What about those teens who don't get asked on dates? Do you know how they feel? Unattractive. Left out. Insignificant.

Our self-image doesn't depend on others, of course. True security comes from knowing God made us and loves us the way we are. Nevertheless, the dating system creates an atmosphere of comparison that makes many teens feel inferior. Some even lie about having a boyfriend or girlfriend at another school or church just to protect their reputation. How sad! And it's totally unnecessary.

Think about Exodus 20:4-6. Do you think it bothers God when we love someone or something else more than him? (See also James 4:4-5)

Loss of spiritual passion. Teens who look to their peers, and especially those of the opposite sex, for a sense of worth and fulfillment are jeopardizing their relationship with the Lord. Your boyfriend or girlfriend becomes your "idol." The one you live for. The focus of your time, thoughts, and desire. Your other relationships—especially your relationship with God—take a back seat to that "special" person in your life. Over time, your spiritual passion decreases and you slowly lose interest in the Lord, his people, and the church.

Friends First

So is it wrong to be attracted to the opposite sex?

Absolutely not! God created you to be attracted to those of the opposite sex. But as we've just discussed, that attraction can be dangerous if not handled wisely. Attraction is a powerful force. Unless teens keep it within biblical boundaries, it can lead to actions that are very wrong indeed.

So what do you do if you feel attracted to someone? You simply share those feelings with God, and—if they continue—with your parents. Your parents can help you deal with the attraction responsibly. They can also monitor it, and point out any ways in which you're being worldly or flirtatious around the person.

The problems begin when you express your attraction *prematurely* to a particular person. Flirting. Competing for his or her attention. Compromising biblical standards by showing inappropriate affection. Focusing on outward appearance rather than inner character. Priding yourself on "getting" this guy or that girl—as if people were toys that you play with and then throw away.

For several years we have had the privilege of leading the youth ministry at a large annual church conference. Last year we did some teaching on this issue of opposite-sex relationships, challenging the teens to evaluate the man-made system of dating in light of biblical principles.

After I (Sheree) finished my session with the girls, an attractive high-schooler approached me to talk.

"Mrs. Phillips," she began. "I've never heard anyone talk about all this before. God has shown me just how selfish and proud I've been about relationships with guys."

"Really?" I responded. "What do you mean?"

"Well, I see now that the biggest reason I wanted attention from guys and wanted to be seen with certain guys

Digging deeper: Read Matthew 28:18-20. Is it harder to obey this command if your time and energy are caught up in dating?

was my pride. I just wanted to impress them and my girl-friends. And having a boyfriend made me feel special and pretty. God wants me to find my security in *him* and to save *my heart* for my husband. I realize that *not* thinking of the guys as brothers has been a real distraction from my relationship with the Lord."

Wow! This young lady got the message. It's not that being friends with those of the opposite sex is wrong or sinful. In fact, opposite-sex friendships can be great! The problems start when the friendship turns into something romantic, and you begin to single that one person out from all the rest.

---

4 Why would a teenager want a boyfriend or girlfriend?

Sadly, even church youth groups are suffering the consequences of "Christian dating." Guys and girls are more concerned with "who likes whom?" than with reaching their generation for Jesus Christ and giving their lives away to serve others.

> **❝** When you give someone your heart, it's different the next time around. You're leery, and in the back of your mind you're thinking, 'I don't want to do this because I don't want to get hurt again.'[9] **❞**
>
> **—Teenager Matt Dotson**

Remember Sarah and Todd from the beginning of this chapter? Well, they had fun ice-skating together. They laughed and held hands and shared some hot chocolate. Sarah was sure he liked her, and hoped he'd ask her out again the following week.

But he didn't. In fact, he took Amy to a movie instead.

Amy and Sarah were friends. Or at least they used to be. For several months Sarah avoided both Amy and Todd.

She found excuses to miss youth meetings. She was embarrassed. She felt silly thinking someone like Todd would actually like someone like her.

Does it really have to be this way?

A Better Way

Hey, here's some good news for you: there *is* a way to avoid the pain of a broken heart and the dangers of premature romantic attraction. But we'll be honest with you. It probably won't win you any popularity contests. It will require self-control over your thoughts and emotions. It will mean saying "no" to certain activities or relationships. And it will cost you your life.

"What? Cost me my *life*! You gotta be kidding!"

Don't worry—it's not going to kill you. But it may force you to think about relationships in a way you never have before.

Jesus was telling us something very important when he said, "Greater love has no one than this, that he lay down his life for his friends" (John 15:13). The life Jesus is talking about here isn't limited to the physical. Laying down our lives includes laying down our opinions. Our preferences. Our needs. Our reputations. Our drive for acceptance and popularity and a sense of importance. All for the sake of our friends.

This is the kind of love Proverbs 17:17 talks about when it says, "A friend loves at all times." Boyfriend/girlfriend love depends on what you look like. Who you know.

HOW TO KEEP YOUR FRIENDSHIP OUT OF THE ROMANTIC ZONE!

■ Communicate early on that your goal for the relationship is "friends only."

■ Make your friend a friend of the whole family.

■ Avoid spending much time alone or on the phone.

■ Avoid topics like your long-term plans for the future. Sharing your hopes and dreams creates a sense of intimacy, and the future suddenly becomes "our future."

■ Confess and overcome any attitude or action that could give others romantic "signals." Be a friend, not a flirt!

■ Avoid "counseling" conversations that breed dependency. If a guy/girl comes to you with problems, direct him/her to an authority for counsel.

■ Girls, watch the way you dress. This greatly affects whether guys view you as a friend or an object to obtain. Be modest!

■ If the other person begins to communicate romantic, more-than-friends feelings, get your parents involved.

■ Guard your heart! If you become attracted to someone, talk to your parents or another mature, Christian adult who can give you biblical advice.[10]

How you act. What your interests are. How you dress. And because teens change their minds frequently, it only lasts as long as the "feelings" are there.

Biblical love is totally different. It isn't controlled by externals like looks, athletic ability, or popularity. Rather, it focuses on what's *inside*. Biblical love doesn't depend on emotions or appearance. Why? Because emotions change. People get pimples. Not everyone is athletic enough to start on the basketball team or make the cheerleading squad. And who can always afford the newest "look" in clothes?

Real love—biblical love—is hard work. It requires patience, forgiveness, and sticking it out when you don't "feel" like it. Loving this way starts with realizing that you're not perfect...and neither is anyone else.

Think about Philippians 2:3-4. If you want to know the secret of fantastic relationships, this is it!

No greater love exists. This is the real thing—not some here-today-and-gone-tomorrow attraction, but an eager commitment to serve others and meet *their* needs instead of your own.

So what's the alternative to dating? Friendship. Treating that guy in the youth group as your older brother. Thinking of the attractive girl in your history class as your younger sister. And being a true friend— even to those who get ignored or rejected by others— rather than selfishly looking for ways to impress the people you admire.

It's easiest to build this kind of friendship in a group setting, where guys and girls are more free to be them- selves. Teens are much less likely to feel pressured into being "romantic" when they are with a group. There's not the same expectation of showing affection as there would be on a date. And—think about it—group settings protect teens from many of the temptations of dating.

---

5 In the space below, list two or three great ideas for group activities with your friends. (Make them so good that dating couples would be jealous!)

■

■

■

Saving For The Future

Teens, someday when you're ready your heavenly Father will show you who that special person is for you. He or she will be *God's* choice. And the joy of the love you share will go beyond your dreams.

Do you want to experience God's best for you? Then save yourself for that one person. Save your emotions and your heart. Save your "I love yous" and your devotion. Save your affection and hand-holding in the mall. When God's will becomes clear and you discover that special person, you will see that it was well worth the wait. And at that point, your parents or pastor can help you find resources that show how to build your relationship during the period leading up to marriage.

> **❝** To console the broken hearts along the way, we tell ourselves that dating is just a social custom, not intended to be serious, and so on. But hearts do get broken as emotional attachments get cast aside.[11] **❞**
>
> **—Connie Marshner**

Yes, it's hard. The teens we know who have chosen not to date have paid a price. They've been misunderstood. They've been left out of activities by friends. They've had to explain their standards to others, only to be ridiculed. They've had to fight the temptation to give in just to be more popular and well-liked. But they have no regrets, because by saying "No!" to worldly ways of relating with the opposite sex, they are experiencing the thrill of radical commitment to Jesus Christ!

Saying "no!" to dating alone isn't enough. Biblical love means you stop thinking of and treating your Christian brothers and sisters in self-seeking, attention-getting ways that grieve the Holy Spirit and turn a church youth group into a dating club.

Pray about this. Talk together as parents and teens. Get to know other young people who enjoy deep friendship more than shallow romance. And get ready for God to use you like never before as one of his heroes in this selfish generation! ■

1. How did your parents view dating when you were a teen?

2. Did you disagree with any points in this study? How so?

3. Is your teen spending too much time with someone of the opposite sex? Not enough time in groups?

4. What relational guidelines does your teen need now?

5. In what specific ways might you monitor and influence your teen's relationships with those of the opposite sex?

**QUESTIONS FOR
TEENS**

1. How did you feel about dating before you read this study? Have your feelings changed?

2. Who do your friends talk about most, God or girlfriends/boyfriends?

3. Are you a flirt or a show-off?

4. Do you need to be alone with someone to get to know him or her?

5. Are there areas where you are *not* treating your Christian friends like brothers and sisters? Be specific.

FACE TO FACE

1. What kind of person would make the ideal spouse?

2. Do you currently have dating relationships? Do you feel God is saying anything about making adjustments?

3. What are some of the symptoms of selfish "love"? How does biblical love act?

4. Discuss what steps might be involved for a friendship to develop into marriage.

5. How can you make your friendships as good as possible?

Answer to Warm-Up
(from page 83): D.) 35%. And now for something really scary...only a few of these couples felt violence was a reason to end the relationship. In fact, one-fourth saw it as "an act of love"! (Source: *Coping With Dating Violence*, by Nancy N. Rue, The Rosen Publishing Group, 1989, p. 9)

An Important Message to Parents

The following study is on sexual purity. We strongly recommend that you read it *before* you share it with your teen. Depending on his or her age, you may feel it would be premature to cover certain material. Or you may want to have a preliminary discussion before you proceed. On the other hand, you may conclude that your teen needs more explicit instruction than we've provided. We're counting on you to discern what's best!

Please don't avoid the material simply because you feel awkward discussing these topics. Our teens are bombarded with sexually suggestive images and materials. If your teen watches TV or interacts with peers in school or in your neighborhood, chances are he or she is already more "informed" than you realize.

Church attendance and professed conversion don't guarantee sexual purity. Many studies have shown that the sexual behavior of churchgoing teens is virtually the same as that of non-churched teens. That's shocking! And it's the main reason we feel this study is so important.

Some of the terms we use may be unfamiliar to your teens, especially the younger ones. They include:

Sex	Birth control
Unwed mother	Sex education
Sensual	Sexual purity
Fornication	Safe sex
"Go all the way"	Romance
Virginity	Homosexuality
"Sexually transmitted diseases"	AIDS
Sexually "suggestive" materials	Promiscuity

We purposely do not define these terms in this study so that you can explain them in the way you think best. However, we suggest you discuss them with your teen in the near future. Depending on his/her age and maturity, a simple definition may suffice. Those of you with older teens will want to have a more detailed discussion, when you can take the opportunity to correct any false or unbiblical information your child has received.

We hope this study helps you and your teen explore this critical area. If you feel the material doesn't meet your child's needs, we advise you to consult with an experienced friend or pastor who can recommend more appropriate resources. ■

R U SURE U R PURE?

BIBLE STUDY   1 Thessalonians 4:1-8

WARM-UP   Which of the following is *most* likely? *Least* likely?

A. Chance that a first-time smoker will become addicted

B. Chance that a student will become nearsighted in college

C. Chance that you had a pizza delivered in the last 60 days

D. Chance of a white Christmas in New York City

E. Chance that a cat will die after falling six stories

F. Chance of getting AIDS through a blood transfusion

(See page 119 for answers)

PERSONAL STUDY   It seemed like a normal day. We had taken our 11-year-old to run some errands. Then it happened. A voice from the back seat broke the silence.

"What does sex mean, Dad?"

"Excuse me?"

"Sex. What does it mean?"

"Why do you ask?"

"Because that bumper sticker said: 'I brake for sexy women.' And I've seen these words before. I was just wondering what it means."

We'd had similar questions before.

At six it was, "Where do babies come from?" "Well, honey, God created a special way for daddies and mommies to make babies. When you get older we'll explain it to you."

At eight came the observation, "I thought only married people had babies. Why is that single lady pregnant?" "Yes, only married people should have babies. But sometimes people make mistakes that we'll talk to you about when you'll be able to understand a little better. But every baby is precious to God, no matter how they get here."

These kinds of explanations were sufficient then. But we knew the day would come when "we'll explain this when you get older" wouldn't work.

It's not that we were afraid to talk about sex with our kids. We just wanted to make sure we chose the right time. And we didn't want to rush it. Some close friends had prematurely brought up the subject with their son. At age 10, Chris just wasn't ready. They found themselves trying to answer questions he hadn't yet asked.

"A 10-year-old wasn't *ready* for it?" you may ask. "Hey, if you wait until then, chances are they've already heard it all from friends or their 'Family Life' teacher at school!"

In many cases, this is true. A lot of children hear about sex from their friends—way before they have the full picture and usually because of something they've read on a bathroom wall, overheard from an older sibling, or seen in a raunchy music video. Or they pick it up in school, where teachers use movies, diagrams, and displays to instruct today's children (as young as kindergarten in some states) about sex and birth control.

"Education is the key," they say.

And yet the teen pregnancy rate has climbed steadily since all this "education" began in the public schools. Take a look at these heartbreaking statistics on young people between ages 15 and 24:

- Since 1970, births to unwed mothers have more than doubled.

- Over one-million unmarried girls get pregnant each year, with over 500,000 choosing to abort their babies.

- Almost half (47%) of all babies born in 1991 were to unwed mothers, the highest proportion ever recorded.

- Only one-fourth (23%) say they are virgins.[1]

Think about Romans 1:22. Today's "experts" on sexuality should read this before airing their opinions!

> The teachers with the most significant and lasting impact on the next generation...are not in the classrooms of Christian universities or even Christian high schools. They are in the kitchens and living rooms of evangelical homes.[2]
>
> —Fran Sciacca

Why the failure? It's largely because kids are learning from sources other than those best qualified to teach them—their parents. Sadly, there are plenty of irresponsible parents who prefer it this way.

But wait a minute—we've left you hanging with an unanswered question.

When our 11-year-old asked about sex, we did what we had always done. We gave a logical, simple answer.

"Well, you see, it's like this," I (Benny) explained.

"Someday you'll be old enough to get a job. When you fill out the application, you'll have to answer a lot of questions about your name, your address, and your education. It'll also ask you what 'sex' you are, meaning are you male (that means a guy) or female (that means a girl.) Do you understand?"

"Yes, sir. But that's not really what the bumper sticker was talking about, Dad. Was it?"

There was no postponing this one. Our almost-a-teenager was letting us know it was "time." We had been expecting it. Praying about it. Getting ready for it. It wasn't a "normal" day. It was THE day.

"No, you're right," I said. "It wasn't. And after the other kids go to bed tonight we'll talk more about this, okay?"

"Okay, Dad."

Silently, we prayed for a memorable conversation that would both inform and inspire our child about this critical issue.

---

1 Which of the following tasks would an average set of parents dread most?

❑ Paying the car insurance bill

❑ Helping their son with a term paper

❑ Wiping up a day's worth of pet accidents

❑ Staying up all night for their daughter's slumber party

❑ Discussing God's view of sex with their teen

❑ Cleaning out the septic tank

For Mature Audiences Only

We're not trying to lure you with this phrase the way advertisers do. We're serious—this study is not for just anyone.

First, it's not for parents who want to delegate the delicate task of sex education to someone else. Dads and moms, our goal throughout this book is to promote helpful discussions and a deepening relationship between you and your teen. This study is the *last* one you want him or her to work through alone. Your teen's attitude about sex is too important. We can only offer the tools for a healthy and helpful dialogue. Don't leave to us—or anyone—the responsibilities God has given you. You may not know all the technical or biological answers, but you have a heart for your child, and want God's best for him or her. Press through the awkwardness and go for it!

Teen—you may not have the option of discussing this with a parent. If that's the case, we still think you can get a lot out of it. But may we offer some advice? Please find some wise and trusted person in your life who can discuss it with you—an older sibling, teacher, pastor, or church youth leader. Just make sure this person is a Christian who will talk straight with you from a biblical perspective. You may feel funny asking. But the person will appreciate your humility and be honored that you asked.

Second, this is not a study for teens who want to hang onto worldly attitudes about sex. You're not going to find any sympathy for your "uncontrollable desires," or permission to be sexually active as long as you don't "go all the way."

Do you really believe Jesus Christ is the Son of God who died to pay for your sins? Have you put your trust in him? Have you asked him to take charge of your life? Do you believe that when you die you'll go to heaven?

"Yes!" you respond. (And if you're not sure, there's some information in the back of this book about how you *can* believe and become a Christian.)

But *why* do you believe these things? If you are a genuinely converted Christian, you believe these things because the Bible says they're true. And you've chosen to put your faith in what the Bible says.

So your salvation rests on the truth of God's Word and your decision to obey it. Right? Exactly!

Well, the Bible covers a lot more than salvation. It teaches us about friendship. Faith. Marriage. Overcoming fear or anger. Knowing God's will for your life. Love. Preparing for the future. Convincing your parents to buy you a new red Jeep for your birthday. (Just kidding—and making sure you're still with us!) Resisting peer pressure. Kindness. Patience.

And sex.

So Do I Qualify?

You've laid your eternal future on the line. You're a Christian because you believe the Bible is true. If it's not, you're believing a lie—a hoax started 2,000 years ago by a bunch of harebrained fishermen. You're deceived and

Digging deeper: Read Proverbs 6:20-23. Parents, if you provide food and clothes for your teens but not biblical teaching, you've neglected to show them "the way to life."

foolish. You'll die thinking you're about to enter into eternity with Jesus…but never go beyond your own grave.

Whoa. This is getting heavy, isn't it? Yes. Because it's time you started wrestling with some things about your relationship with God and your obedience to his Word. You're not a little kid anymore. This is a part of the "growing up" process we talked about in Study Four.

Growing up requires knowing what you believe and standing by it. Even when it's not the "popular" opinion. Even if all your friends disagree. (Even your *Christian* friends. Not all Christians agree on everything, you know. And just because someone is in your youth group doesn't necessarily mean he or she has biblical convictions on things.) Even when you're ridiculed or rejected. Accused of being old-fashioned. Thought of as weird because you have *not* made it your biggest goal in life to "get" a certain guy or girl.

Standing alone means just that. You're alone. Sometimes God will bring people along to stand with you. As you take a stand for what's right, others may gain the courage to join you. But there's no guarantee.

That's why this study is for mature audiences only. And you're still trying to figure out whether or not you qualify.

How old are you? "Hey, I'm not a kid anymore. I'm almost a young adult!" Maturity has little to do with age. We've known 12-year-olds who were a lot more mature than many 18-year-olds.

How much do you know? "I have an A- average and I know a lot of the Bible." Doing well in school doesn't count, either. Just because you're smart or know a lot of memory verses doesn't mean you're *wise*.

Do others respect you? "I don't mean to brag, but all my friends look up to me." Makes no difference. There are plenty of immature people who are respected for foolish reasons, like what kind of car they drive or the labels on their clothes.

> **❝** Youth is the seed-time of full age, the molding season in the little space of human life, the turning point in the history of man's mind.
>
> By the shoot we judge of the tree, by the blossom we judge of the fruit, by the spring we judge of the harvest, by the morning we judge of the day, and by the character of the young man, we may generally judge what he will be when he grows up.
>
> Young man [or woman], do not be deceived. Do not think you can willfully serve your self and your pleasures in the beginning of life, and then go and serve God with ease at the end.[3] **❞**
>
> —J.C. Ryle

Think about Psalm 119:97. If you learn to love God's commands like this, you'll have no trouble standing alone.

2 What do *you* think makes a person mature? Before reading any further, write your answer below.

Let's look at a part of the Bible that tells us a lot about maturity. And let's read it with sexual purity in mind.

We have much to say about this *[and as you'll see, we do!]*, but it is hard to explain because you are slow to learn *[nothing personal, but so true of many Christian teens today]*. In fact, though by this time you ought to be teachers *[of your peers]*,…you *[still]* need milk, not solid food! Anyone who lives on milk, being still an infant *[spiritually and emotionally, that is]*, is not acquainted with the teaching about righteousness. But solid food is for the *mature*, who *by constant use have trained themselves to distinguish good from evil* (Hebrews 5:11-14, comments and emphasis added).

Think about Hebrews 12:1-3. How does the example set by Jesus encourage you to persevere on the path toward maturity?

This passage says four major things about maturity.

First, it won't come to the lazy. Especially to those who are "slow to learn" (verse 11)—such as teens who don't act on truth until *they* figure it's right for them. Or until they have had their fun and feel "old" enough to get serious about God.

Second, it's not for the childish (verse 13). Imagine a 10-year-old walking around still drinking a bottle. It's just as juvenile for teenagers who have been taught the things of God still to be living on the stuff you learned in toddler Sunday School. It's time to mature.

Third, it requires perseverance (verse 14). Over time and through "constant use" the immature Christian gains maturity. Hoping to become a skilled pianist won't make it happen. Only years of consistent, sometimes exhausting practice will. The same is true of Christian maturity.

And, fourth, it involves taking responsibility for yourself (verse 14). Godly role models and discipleship will help. But the truly mature are those who have "trained themselves." Your parents or others can instruct and warn you about things. But they usually won't be around when the temptation hits. In that moment, your "maturity" is tested when only God is watching.

Are you ready to overcome laziness? Are you willing to persevere and take responsibility for yourself? Can you handle some radical talk about sex from a purely biblical perspective?

Then read on.

The Instructions Are All In The Manual

The night we had "the talk" with our 11-year-old we read a book together (which is unfortunately out of print). It talked about weddings. When a couple gets married, it explained, people bring them gifts. Towels. A toaster. Maybe a silver platter or some candle holders. On that day God gives them a gift, too. It's called sex.

This helped our child see that sex was God's idea. He invented it. After he had created all kinds of living things, God made Adam "in his own image." Despite millions of different animals, "no suitable helper was found" for Adam.

In other words, the hippos and camels and giraffes were cool. But none of them did a whole lot for Adam. Romantically speaking, that is.

Then God made Eve.

When he saw *her*, Adam said: "This is now bone of my bone and flesh of my flesh; she shall be called 'woman.'" In more contemporary terms he was saying, "YES! *She's* exactly what I've been looking for. Way to go, God!"

God then told them to "Be fruitful and multiply." And though it's just a guess, we bet he had to give them some pointers. That would mean *God* conducted the first sex education class in history! Soon after, Adam and Eve conceived their first son, Cain. (You can read all about this in Genesis 1 through 4. Specific references are from 1:27-28; 2:19-20, 23; 4:1).

If, as many suggest, God is some anti-sex, steal-the-fun Scrooge, why would he have made it *the* way for couples to have children? He knew from the beginning that sexual intimacy would bring pleasure. And that's the way he wanted it.

Digging deeper: Read Psalm 37:4 and 1 Timothy 6:17. God tells us to avoid counterfeit pleasures only because he wants us to experience the *ultimate* pleasure!

May your fountain be blessed and may you rejoice in the wife *[not the girlfriend or boyfriend]* of your youth…May her affections satisfy you always. May you ever be captivated *["intoxicated" in some translations]* by her love (Proverbs 5:18,19).

Yes, sex within marriage can bring joy and tremendous satisfaction. But sex outside marriage is sin. It may feel pleasurable at first, but it will ultimately cause great heartache and trouble.

> **Purity means freedom from contamination, from anything that would spoil the taste or the pleasure, reduce the power, or in any way adulterate what the thing was meant to be. It means cleanness, clearness—no additives, nothing artificial—in other words, 'all natural,' in the sense in which the Original Designer designed it to be.**[4]
>
> **—Elisabeth Elliot**

Sex is a lot like fire. In the right place and at the right time, fire is a great thing. It warms us in the fireplace. It cooks our food. It makes the water hot for our showers. It sends rockets into space and beautiful colors into the sky on the Fourth of July.

But it can also burn a family's home to the ground. Or heat the heroin that is shot into an addict's veins. Or blacken hundreds of thousands of once-beautiful forestland.

Sexuality, too, is a beautiful thing. But if unmarried couples think they can play with matches and not get burned, they are headed for disaster.

Suppose two people buy the same kind of stereo system. In bold letters on both boxes is written: FOLLOW THE MANUFACTURER'S INSTRUCTIONS CLOSELY TO AVOID ELECTRICAL MALFUNCTION.

One takes the box home. Carefully reads and follows the instructions. Takes the time to check and re-check each step. And in three hours he's lying on the couch listening to his new CD player. (Sure, the salesman said it would only take an hour. No big deal, though.) Later he gets on the phone and invites some friends over to check out his new system.

The other guy takes his box home. Pulls everything out. Lets the instructions fall on the floor, untouched. (Hey, he never reads instructions. It's just a waste of time.) Unaware that some of the electrical components are different than the old stereo he put together 10 years ago, he quickly hooks it up and plugs it in. Less than an hour after he started he's lying on the couch, eyes closed, listening to his music.

But then he smells something. Smoke. Black clouds are billowing out of his receiver! He, too, gets on the phone—but his call is to the fire department.

One followed the manufacturer's instructions. The other didn't. He was too proud. Too confident he could "handle it." Too impatient.

God is the manufacturer of sexual intimacy. Therefore, he has the wisdom and right to decide who should use it. When to use it. And how to enjoy it. The instructions are all clearly explained in his manual, the Bible. And there are some significant warnings about what happens to those who are too proud, confident, and in a hurry to follow them.

God blesses those who choose to follow his ways. But those who don't will suffer the consequences.

---

3 "There is no such thing as *free* love or *free* sex," write Josh McDowell and Dick Day. "Someone always pays for promiscuity...."

Here's a shocking example. On average, how much do you think federal and state governments spend on costs related to *one* teenage pregnancy?

(Answer printed upside down at bottom of page)

"What He Doesn't Know Won't Hurt Me..."

It hasn't been *that* long since we were teenagers. We remember thinking we had gotten away with some things. Like the drive-in incident.

Sheree's mom didn't approve of drive-in movie theaters. (For those of you too young to know about them, ask your parents.) She insisted that "no daughter of hers would go to such a place alone with a boy." A lot of teens and their dates went to the drive-in not so much because of the movie, but because they could be alone together.

But we just wanted to watch "The Ten Commandments."

No kidding! By this point, we were both Christians. Drive-ins usually showed the kind of movies Christians didn't see. So we couldn't believe it when we heard "The Ten Commandments" was playing. We didn't mention it to Mom because she "wouldn't understand." Besides, no one would know and we'd never go back again.

The next day Mom asked us where we'd been. We said we had seen "The Ten Commandments" at the movies

Answer: For every teen who has a child out of wedlock, medical and welfare costs average 100,000 dollars! (Source: The Associated Press, quoted in Josh McDowell and Dick Day, *Why Wait?* (San Bernardino, CA: Here's Life Publishers, ©1987), p. 47.

(not really a lie—just not the whole truth). More questions came, and we could tell she wasn't happy. After several minutes of our trying to avoid telling *her* the truth, she told it to *us*.

"I know you went to the drive-in last night," she said. "Your aunt was there and saw you go into the snack bar."

We tried to explain, but it didn't do any good. Mom was upset and disappointed.

Why is this such a big deal? we thought. *We just wanted to see a wholesome movie together. And now a nosy aunt and an overprotective mother are treating us like a couple of sneaky, teenage rebels.*

Like many teens, we were blaming others instead of learning what God wanted to teach *us* from this experience. The problem was a simple one. Confident of our ability to handle the situation, we had decided to bend the rule "just this once." No one would ever find out. There would be no consequences. We'd have a fun night together and go on with our lives.

Think about 1 Corinthians 10:12.
Often it's when we think we're invincible that we're most vulnerable!

This reasoning would sound all too familiar to the hundreds of thousands of teenage girls who will become pregnant this year. Or the many heartbroken Christian teens who will give in to "get a boyfriend or girl-friend"—and then get dumped for someone else in the youth group.

Our drive-in experience taught us a very important lesson. Pride and compromise are serious to God.

> ❝ Premarital sex gave me fear as a gift...and shame to wear as a garment. It stole my peace of mind and robbed me of hope in a bright future. Sex smashed my concentration in class to smithereens. My desire for church activities was ground to a pulp. It made crumbs of the trust I had known in Christ...and in men and women. Sex gave me a jagged tear in my heart that even now, seven years later, is still healing.[5] ❞
>
> **—Name Withheld**

Because we had yielded to temptation once, God knew we were likely to do it again, with the possibility of more serious consequences. So in his kindness, he saw to it that we were exposed.

God may expose you through an aunt who "happens" to be at the same drive-in movie theater. A teacher who "happens" to look up just as you're checking your cheat sheet. A parent who "happens" to walk into the room just when the four-letter word pops out of your mouth. And even when you think you're getting away with sin because no one "happens" to see or hear, remember this: God always sees and always hears. He is omnipresent (everywhere at the same time) and omniscient (all-knowing).

He is also omnipotent (all-powerful) and will discipline you when you rebel against his standards.

The following scriptures soberly warn us not to think we can hide things from such a God:

> 'Can anyone hide in secret places so that I cannot see him?' declares the Lord (Jeremiah 23:24).

> For God will bring every deed into judgment, including every hidden thing, whether it is good or evil (Ecclesiastes 12:14).

> You have set our iniquities before you, our secret sins in the light of your presence (Psalm 90:8).

> There is nothing concealed that will not be disclosed, or hidden that will not be made known (Luke 12:2).

> He will bring to light what is hidden in darkness (1 Corinthians 4:5).

"What he doesn't know won't hurt me" is the lie too many Christian teens believe about God. Yet he knows and sees all. No matter where you are, who you are with, or what you're thinking or doing, God is there. Not because he's waiting to squelch your "fun" or hit you over the head if you sin, but because he's your loving Father. He knows what's best for you. He wants to protect and help you. He has a wonderful future for you—and he doesn't want you to mess it up with foolish mistakes.

Ten Questions Teens Ask

We said we would be straight with you. So now's the time to get into some specific issues about sexuality. Below are our responses to the 10 questions Christian teens most often ask about sex. Teens, you may have some very specific questions that we won't answer. Or you may be tempted in a certain way we don't address. If so, discuss it honestly with your parents. Don't let embarrassment hold you back. The only stupid question is the one that's never asked.

Are you saying it's wrong for me to be attracted to the opposite sex? Definitely not! God designed you to experience this attraction. Guys notice girls; girls notice guys. And it's normal to want to be attractive to others. The problems come when attraction becomes a *distraction* and you find yourself wanting to give and receive emotions and affection that God has reserved for marriage.

Isn't sex okay as long as you love the person and are "safe"? No! The Bible is clear on this important issue: sexual intimacy and pleasure are for *married couples only*. "For the Christian," writes Elisabeth Elliot, "there is one rule and one rule only: total abstention from sexual activity outside of marriage and total faithfulness inside marriage. Period."[6] Using birth control—what people call "safe sex"—may prevent disease or pregnancy (although it's no guarantee). But there's no such thing as "safe" sex outside of marriage.

Digging deeper: If you want to read some of the main Bible passages that outline God's rules for sexuality, see Exodus 20:14; Romans 1:24-32; 1 Corinthians 6:9-10; Galatians 5:19-21; and Ephesians 5:31.

The Bible calls any sexual involvement before marriage *fornication*, and it leaves no room for excuses. No blaming the other person for talking you into something you didn't really want to do (nobody can "make" you sin!). No defending yourself because things "got out of hand" before you realized what was happening. Fornication is sin and the only appropriate responses are to *run* from it (1 Corinthians 6:18) or *repent* of it (1 John 1:9).

Love is not the condition for sexual involvement. *Marriage* is. And besides, feelings of love or attraction come and go, especially during the teen years.

One more thought on this point: Those who favor "safe" sex talk about it as if sex were only physical, and preventing pregnancy or disease were the only concerns. But sexual intimacy is emotional as well. Those who truly want to practice "safe" sex will be just as careful to guard themselves from the pain of a broken heart or the shame of a shattered reputation.

---

4 Which of the following do you think would be appropriate between a young man and woman who (A) really love God but (B) are *not* serious about marriage?

(Answer printed upside down at bottom of next page.)

☐ Holding hands

☐ Group activities

☐ Kissing

☐ Long phone conversations

☐ Going on a date

☐ Talking about marriage

☐ Sharing personal secrets

☐ Writing romantic cards/notes

☐ Serving on the youth planning team

☐ Visiting each other's families

Why does God forbid sex before marriage? Why do highway builders put guardrails on mountain roads? To keep fools from driving off cliffs and killing themselves! God's laws about sex are given to protect you. Just as drugs, alcohol, or nicotine can destroy you physically and emotionally, so can sexual uncleanness (any sexual involvement outside of marriage). Only a fool would ignore the signs.

But there's an even greater reason to remain pure until marriage. Look carefully at the following verses:

> **"** Skilled drivers know that when driving on a mountain road, the best place to focus is not on the guardrails at the edge of the cliff; the best place to focus is on the center line. If you're worried about falling over the edge of the cliff when it comes to your relationships with members of the opposite sex, quit looking at the guardrail—'how far you can go'; keep your eye on the center line: God's purpose for your life and relationships.[7] **"**
>
> **—John Holzmann**

Flee from sexual immorality...he who sins sexually, sins against his own body. Do you not know that your body is a temple of the Holy Spirit, who is in you, whom you have received from God? You are not your own; you were bought at a price. Therefore, honor God with your body (1 Corinthians 6:18-20).

Sexual sin defiles the very dwelling place ("temple") of the God of the universe...YOU!

As a Christian, you belong to God. Your body should be a holy temple where the holy God can feel at home. It's best for you. And it honors the One who made you.

Is it okay to be affectionate with someone as long as we don't "go all the way?" Imagine for a minute that you're sitting at the top of a long, slippery water slide. For the moment you still have a choice. Should you climb back down while you can (even if the others in line laugh at you) or should you push yourself over the edge?

You cautiously inch your way onto the slide. But once you start moving, it becomes harder and harder to stop, and within seconds you are hurtling off the end of the slide and into the water.

Sexual sin works the same way. It's not the bottom of the slide that's dangerous. It's the top. "The way of sin is down hill," said British church leader Robert Leighton to an earlier generation. "A man cannot stop whenever he wishes."[8] "Innocent" things like kissing (and other forms of affection your parents may want to discuss with you)

Answer: We're not interested in giving a list of "dos and don'ts." What's important here is the *principle*. Young people should avoid any activity or situation that fuels romantic affection or sexual desire. By focusing on friendship rather than romance, teens will spare themselves a lot of pressure...and gain a better sense of what's most important for a successful marriage.

113

Digging deeper: Read Proverbs 7:6-23. This young man went down the slippery slide…and it cost him his life.

create thoughts and often lead to actions that become nearly impossible to control.

Remember our last study? You are to treat members of the opposite sex as your brothers or sisters in Christ (1 Timothy 5:2). Anything you wouldn't do with your sibling is "off limits" with your peers. Your conscience (that blinking red light on the dashboard of your heart) will often let you know when you're thinking of or treating someone in an inappropriate way. (Unless you have ignored the warning light so long that it has burned out.)

There will be plenty of time for giving and receiving romantic affection when you are married. As the Bible tells us, "There is a time for everything, and a season for every activity under heaven…a time to embrace and a time to refrain…He has made everything beautiful *in its time*" (Ecclesiastes 3:1,5,11, emphasis added).

Those who rush prematurely into emotional or physical affection pay a hefty price, both now and in the future.

What *are* the problems that can come from teen sex? Here's a list of some of the most obvious dangers:

Loss of virginity	Pregnancy
Forced marriage	Abortion
Sexually transmitted diseases	Death from AIDS
Divorce	Single parenthood
Depression	Guilt
Physical and emotional side effects of abortion	

As frightening as these are, they would affect you only in this life. But the spiritual consequences can be eternal. We have watched too many teens sacrifice God's call and plan for their life for some quick thrills with a date.

In Romans 8:35, we find a long list of things that cannot separate us from God's love. But *one* thing can. It's found in Isaiah 59:2: "…your iniquities have separated you from your God; your sins have hidden his face from you." If you rebel against God's clear standards, your relationship with him will suffer.

Separation from God is a serious thing. Don't let it happen to you.

I've heard a lot about homosexuality. Does the Bible say anything about it? Yes, it does. Homosexuality is not an "alternative lifestyle" as you may have heard. God's Word clearly describes it as unnatural and sinful. Marriage and sex are reserved for opposite-sex couples only. Your parents would know the best way to answer any other questions you may have on this subject.

Digging deeper: Homosexuality is clearly outlawed by the Bible. (See Leviticus 18:22 and Romans 1:24-27)

114

Think about 1 Corinthians 13:5. If someone claims to love you but pressures you to show physical affection, it isn't real love.

How can I expect to keep a boyfriend/girlfriend if I'm not affectionate with him/her? This question suggests you need to go back to Study Six. People are not possessions to "get" or "have" or "keep." We are beings created by a loving and merciful God for *his* use and glory. We belong to him and him alone!

Do you feel pressured to "have" a boyfriend or "get" a girlfriend? If so, this pressure certainly doesn't come from God. He has a much better way for you to relate with the opposite sex. Stop concerning yourself with your reputation and simply be a friend. (We believe you'll find it's a lot more fun!)

---

5 Wow! You're judging the annual "Fool of the Year" competition. Which of these teens deserves the gold?

Drew: Wasted a month's allowance on video games

Cindy: Lost her driver's license after getting three tickets

Ralph: Thought he could pass Geometry by sleeping on his textbook

Louise: Fell for 17 "April Fool" jokes in one day

Robert: Stuck his tongue to an ice cube tray

Sheila: Thought sex would make her more popular

But I'm in love with this person. What do I do with these feelings? Often teens find themselves strongly attracted to someone. You think about, dream of, and eagerly look forward to seeing this special person. You notice certain things about him or look for reasons to talk about her with your friends. You brush your teeth extra hard and wear extra perfume or cologne when he or she will be around. Strong feelings swirl around in your heart and head. And many teens feel they must *express* these feelings verbally and physically.

> **❝** When we begin to develop intimacy with someone, there's going to be a natural tendency toward a sexual expression... Any time you become emotionally involved with a person, you're moving into the arena of sexual temptation.[9] **❞**
>
> **—Burdette Palmberg**

If this is you, don't be embarrassed. But you need to get a grip on these feelings and begin thinking of this person

Think about Romans 8:9. Do you ever feel "out of control" of your feelings or actions? This verse shows you who *is* in control!

as your brother or sister in Christ. Romantic affections *begin* with romantic thoughts. Not controlling how you think can quickly lead to sin.

Your safeguard is to grow in self-control (Galatians 5:22-24). Throughout your life you'll be tempted to do things you should not do. Begin now to say "no" to those desires before you act on them. The more you exercise the "muscle" of self-control, the stronger it will become.

In addition, get up the courage to tell your parents or another wise Christian what you're feeling. Chances are very good they felt the same way when they were your age. Their counsel and prayer will help keep you from sinful attitudes or actions. And God will help you, too!

I've already sinned in this area. I'm feeling bad and confused. What should I do? Again, you need to talk to someone who can wisely walk you through the process of repentance and change. There is no sexual sin God won't forgive. No matter how badly you've failed, his love and cleansing are available to you. But you have to be serious enough to turn from your sin and take whatever steps are necessary to avoid repeating it. A quick "God, please forgive me" won't do it.

The Bible says, "If we confess *[agree with God about]* our sins, he is faithful and just to forgive us our sins and purify *[completely cleanse]* us from all unrighteousness" (1 John 1:9, comments added). Agree with God about your sin. It was wrong and selfish. It grieved him. And now you see it.

Whether you talk to a parent or someone else, make sure you fully understand the following:

■ How to experience genuine repentance

■ What steps to take so that you don't repeat the sin

■ What to communicate to the person or people you sinned against

How do I avoid being tempted in this area? Great question! Even if you don't date, certain things can cause you to be sexually stimulated or tempted. Here are some you'll want to pray about and discuss with your parents:

Sexually suggestive movies, TV shows, or videos. Don't depend on the "rating" system or recommendations from your friends. We suggest that parents preview all media materials before approving them for teens. Sound a little "overprotective"? Not if you consider the price your teen may have to pay if they see something that leads them into sin.

TV commercials. Keep the remote control nearby when watching TV. Advertisers know that sex sells. Even "safe"

shows include raunchy and suggestive commercials. These images are hard for teens to erase from their minds.

Magazines. The "adult" ones are clearly off limits. But don't be deceived. Even teen magazines, women's magazines, and "guy" magazines (camping, fishing, weightlifting, etc.) have suggestive advertisements and articles.

Sports section of the newspaper. Parents, we can't just hand the sports page to our teenage sons anymore. Marketers know that men are the primary readers of the sports section. We recently contacted our local paper about running two highly visible ads *on the same day*. The ads included pictures and explicit language promoting certain "products."

Books. Much of what is advertised as "wholesome" teen reading is romantic in nature. Girls are especially drawn to these books and novels, which talk about relationships in ways that stir up a premature interest in romance.

Romantic fantasies. Teens, if you let it, your imagination will speed out of control. Exercise that muscle of self-control by refusing to entertain thoughts about romance, or wondering what it would be like to show your affection to someone in more than a friendly way. (Read and memorize Philippians 4:8 to combat such thoughts.) Remind yourself to think of your peers as brothers and sisters in Christ. Period.

Parents, take the initiative to talk with your teen and see if he or she is tempted in this area. (Some are, some aren't.)

Immodest clothing. You may not realize it, but clothing that shows off your body can tempt others to think about you in the wrong way. Christian teens should stand out in the crowd, especially during the summers—not because of their neon bathing suits, but because of their modesty! Don't dress to get attention. And avoid being with or looking at those who dress immodestly.

Because of the world we live in, you'll never be able to avoid all of these all the time. Even if you could, it wouldn't guarantee that you would never be sexually tempted. But being wise about what you see, hear, and think will certainly help.

Digging deeper: By faithfully guarding your eyes and thoughts, you will have won half the battle against sin. (See Psalm 101:3 and 119:37; Proverbs 4:25-27; and Isaiah 33:15-16)

> **❝** Our bodies are not our own. They belong to God. We need God's permission to do anything with them. This is the radical Christian stance on sexuality: it does not exist merely to aid and abet in the pursuit of pleasure, but primarily to glorify God. This is why we cannot buy into the 'If it feels good, do it' mindset. Our mindset, rather, must be, 'If it glorifies God, do it.' And only in faithful, fruitful Christian marriage do we find what glorifies God.[10] **❞**
>
> **—Connie Marshner**

Counting The Cost Of Purity

As you can tell, this is the longest study in the book. We've tried to address some of your questions and talk straight with you about the Bible's view of sex. Now it's time for *you* to make the choice. Will you have the courage to live God's way? Will you walk in purity among a generation of teens living blindly for themselves? Will you be wise enough to avoid the tragedy of sexual sin?

The costs will seem high. You'll have to deal honestly and biblically with temptation. At times marriage will seem like an eternity away. Situations may arise when you have to stand alone on your convictions. You'll probably be misunderstood by some of your friends, perhaps even rejected. But as God helped King David, he will also help you: "The arrogant mock me without restraint; but I *do not* turn from your law" (Psalm 119:51, emphasis added).

Pray about it. Talk it over with your parents. And then join the emerging army of other outstanding teens like yourself in making the following pledge to walk in purity.

R U sure U R pure?

May the cry of your heart and the fruit of your life be a resounding **YES!**

MY PLEDGE OF PURITY

"Flee the evil desires of your youth,
and pursue righteousness, faith,
love and peace, along with those who
call on the Lord out of a pure heart."
(2 Timothy 2:22)

I desire to glorify Jesus Christ in my teenage years by obeying his standards for holy living. By the grace and power of God, I commit myself this day to walk in sexual purity. With his strength, I will exercise self-control in my relationships with those of the opposite sex and I will remain pure for my future spouse.

Signed _____

Date _____

Witnessed by _____

QUESTIONS FOR PARENTS

1. Who is your child's primary source of information about sexuality? (A) Friends, (B) Media, (C) Youth leader, (D) Yourself, (E) Teachers, (F) Other.

2. Do any past sins or experiences keep you from talking openly about this subject?

3. What further direction, if any, do you need to give your child at this time regarding sexuality?

4. Do you view sex in marriage as positively as God does?

5. How can you help your teen avoid temptation?

QUESTIONS FOR TEENS

1. What questions do you have after reading this study?

2. Are you comfortable talking to your parents about sex?

3. How can this gift from God be so beautiful and dangerous at the same time?

4. What's the first thing you should do if you get into a tempting situation? (Hint: See 1 Corinthians 6:18)

5. Who has most real freedom, the sexually active or the sexually pure?

FACE TO FACE

1. Discuss any terms in this study you didn't understand.

2. Why does God command us to save sex for marriage?

3. Discuss your answers to Question 4 on page 112.

4. Talk and pray together about the emotional/physical boundaries you think should guard a relationship.

5. Of the temptations mentioned near the end of this study (magazines, romantic fantasies, etc.), which tempt you?

6. How can we work together to keep this pledge of purity?

Answer to Warm-Up
(from page 101): It's *most* likely that the first-time cigarette user will become addicted (nine in ten do). Thanks to the screening and testing procedures used by the Red Cross, it's *least* likely that you would get AIDS from a transfusion. The risk is only one in 225,000! The Red Cross makes sure it is pure! (Source: American Red Cross; *What Counts: The Complete Harper's Index.*

WANNABES NEED NOT APPLY

BIBLE STUDY   1 Corinthians 9:24-25

WARM-UP   Though many teens admire professional basketball players, few will ever make it in the NBA themselves. Of the 20.5 million American teens, how many will…

■ Buy one of Champion's NBA team jerseys?

■ Play on an NCAA college basketball team?

■ Be drafted by the NBA after college?

(See page 135 for answer)

PERSONAL STUDY   "If I could be like Mike."

This commercial slogan expressed the secret desire of young people all across America during the record-setting career of basketball great Michael Jordan. Bald and tongue-wagging, he captured the heart and imagination of a generation of wannabes.

"If I could dunk like Mike. Get a crowd cheering like Mike. Leap from the foul line and fly like Mike. Make money like Mike. Be famous and respected like Mike."

Author Dallas Willard talks about this kind of wishful thinking in his book *The Spirit of the Disciplines*. He describes the effort teens put into imitating their favorite baseball player:

The star is well known for sliding head first into bases, so the teenagers do too. The star holds his bat above his head, so the teenagers do too. These young people try anything and everything their idol does, hoping to be like him—they buy the type of shoes the star wears, the same glove he uses, the same bat.

Will they succeed in performing like the star, though? We all know the answer quite well. We know that they won't succeed if all they do is try to be like him in the game—no matter how gifted they may be in their own way. And we all understand why. The star performer himself didn't achieve his excellence by trying to behave in a certain way *only during the game.* Instead, he chose an overall life of preparation of mind and body, pouring all his energies into that total preparation....[1]

Wanting to be like Michael Jordan isn't enough. Try shaving your head. Dangling your tongue while you're on the court. Wearing North Carolina shorts under your uniform and a knee brace below your knee. It probably won't help. Even though you have a good outside shot, a nice dribble, make occasional spin moves to the basket or finger roll lay ups...one day you'll have to admit it.

You aren't really like Mike.

Jordan has plenty of natural athletic ability. But he didn't become a star just by showing up for the games to show off his "natural abilities." It took lots of hard work. Hours and hours of practice when he felt like doing other things. So when game time came, he was ready. Ready to dribble and dunk and pass and soar. Millions saw him shine on national television. But few ever saw what took place between games—the sweat, the drills, and the workouts that really made him what he was.

Many of today's churchgoing teens are "wannabe" Christians. They want to be godly. Respected for their beliefs. Able to resist temptation and sin. And yet when that moment of temptation comes, they regularly cave in to compromise.

Maybe you're one of them. You don't want to show disrespect to your parents. You don't want to treat your younger sister unkindly. You don't want to give in to the pressure to conform to the world.

But you do.

Think about James 1:22-25. Don't waste your time talking or thinking about being a Christian. Just do it!

---

1 Think back over the last few days...things you've said and done (or *not* done). Is there anything you feel bad about or wish you could do over?

Others have felt the same inner struggle—including the apostle Paul. Do his comments sound familiar?

I do not understand my own actions—I am baffled, bewildered. I do not accomplish what I wish, but I do the very thing that I loathe…I can will what is right, but I cannot perform it—I have the intention and urge to do what is right, but no power to carry it out; for I fail to practice the good deeds I desire to do, but the evil deeds that I do not desire to do are what I am doing (Romans 7:15, 18-19; Amplified Bible).

Maybe you submitted your life to Jesus as a kid. Or perhaps you had a "mountain top" experience at last year's youth retreat, when you tearfully recommitted your life to follow him. You may be actively involved in a church and regularly attend the youth meetings.

But when game time comes, you choke.

The game is on-the-court living. Those clutch moments when you find what you're really made of as a Christian. Times when the real you pops out. And no matter how powerful your experience was at last year's retreat, unless you are practicing things like patience and humility and self-control, you're gonna choke when the pressure is on.

> **44** Discipline is the price of freedom. **77**
>
> —Elton Trueblood

Digging deeper: What nine things *should* pop out of us when we're under pressure? (See Galatians 5:22)

Do you give in when tempted to lie to your parents? Cheat on a test? Use profanity? Yell at your brother? Flirt with that nice-looking guy? Gossip about a friend?

You can *want* to do the right thing until you're blue in the face. But regularly giving in to temptation "on the court" means you haven't been paying the price in daily practice *off* the court. That's where stars are made.

Training For An Audience Of One

I (Sheree) played the piano when I was young. Every spring my instructor had all her students perform a recital. It was the highlight of the year. Our family and friends would come to see the results of a year of practice and study.

I enjoyed playing the piano. But I didn't like the practice. Eleven months out of the year Mom frequently had to remind me to get out the music and play. During the month before the recital, though, I practiced so much I think even Mom got tired of hearing me. Why? Because my reputation was at stake. I wasn't about to show up at the recital and make a fool of myself like my friend Liz. (One year she ended up stopping in the middle of a song, humiliated and in tears because she hadn't practiced enough. Not me!)

Trying to impress others is a pretty poor reason to practice. Unless you're willing to persevere, you'll never be a peak performer. I can't play much on the piano today because I only took it seriously for one month out of the year. No recital, no diligence.

Digging deeper: Read 1 Corinthians 4:2-5. Did Paul worry about impressing others? His only goal was to please God!

As a teen, your motive for playing well in the game of life should be to please and honor God. The true test of your maturity as a Christian isn't how you do in up-front situations when others are watching or when your parents are around. Nor is it reflected in the opinions of those who only see you on Sunday mornings. Maturity is who you are when there's no one else around. No friends to impress. No parents to obey. Just you...and an audience of One.

> ❝ Live as in the sight of God....*Do* nothing you would not like God to see. *Say* nothing you would not like God to hear. *Write* nothing you would not like God to read. *Go* to no place where you would not like God to find you. *Read* no book of which you would not like God to say, 'Show it to me.' Never spend your time in such a way that you would not like to have God say, 'What are you doing?'[2] ❞
>
> **—J.C. Ryle**

That's why the Bible teaches that radical commitment to Christ isn't for wannabes. It's for those who don't just *want* to know and follow God, but who are willing to put in the time and effort to make it happen.

Basketball wasn't big in Paul's day, but track and field was. Listen to what he says about the way first-century runners competed (we've added a few comments, too):

Do you not know that in a race all the runners run, but only one gets the prize? Run in such a way as to get the prize. *[Don't just settle for a lukewarm, mediocre relationship with the Lord!]* Everyone who competes goes into strict training *[notice these words—it requires hard work and diligence]*. They do it to get a crown that will not last *[yes, even Michael Jordan's accomplishments on the court will mean nothing in eternity]*; but we do it to get a crown that will last forever (1 Corinthians 9:24-25).

Don't Worry, Be Holy

American Christians find it pretty easy to think of God as a loving Father. When we read about his promise of abundant life (John 10:10), we hold out both hands and expect the best. But here's a bit of a shocker: God isn't very concerned about your happiness.

(Read that sentence again—it's an important one.)

Think about Matthew 5:11-12. If happiness was your goal, you'd have a hard time obeying this command!

God loves and cares for you more than you will ever know, but he isn't pacing heaven wondering how good you feel. That's because his goal for you isn't happiness—it's *holiness*. Happiness is an emotion that comes from things like shopping for a new outfit or hitting a home run in the bottom of the ninth. Holiness is a way of living that comes from "strict training" to be like Jesus.

Happiness is living for the weekend. Holiness is living for eternity.

If happiness is *your* goal, then Christianity isn't for you. But if you're willing to walk in the way of holiness, read on. It may not always make you happy, but it will fill you with joy.

---

2 In your opinion, which of these song titles from the past best sums up the Christian life?

❏ "Don't Worry, Be Happy"

❏ "Working For The Weekend"

❏ "The Long And Winding Road"

❏ "I Feel Good"

❏ "For Your Eyes Only"

❏ "Jesus Is Just Alright With Me"

❏ "Stairway To Heaven"

The "D" Word

Growing in holiness is described in the Bible by the word "sanctification." (You remember this term from Study Two.) Simply defined, sanctification is the lifelong process of becoming spiritually mature. Justification, on the other hand, happens the moment you are born again. At conversion you are *justified*—because his Son died to pay the price for your sin, God declares you righteous.

You begin as a "baby Christian," but over the years you learn how to think and respond as a mature believer. You grow in Christ-like character. You become more responsible. You are being sanctified!

But it's a lot easier to get happy than it is to get sanctified. Why? Because sanctification requires something that is foreign to the vocabulary of many Christians: *discipline*.

> **"** Though the power for godly character comes from Christ, the responsibility for developing and displaying that character is ours.[3] **"**
> —**Jerry Bridges**

You don't often see the "D" word on bumper stickers or in birthday cards. How many college students do you think would sign up voluntarily for a "Discipline 101" class? And when you were younger, did you respond eagerly when your dad announced he needed to "discipline" you?

No. Discipline isn't a popular word. And yet it's the path to holiness. The serious Christian teen doesn't just endure discipline—he or she welcomes and embraces it.

If you're involved in a church, you've probably heard the term "spiritual disciplines." It describes those things that help us in the sanctification process. Serious athletes rely on *physical* disciplines like weightlifting or running. They train consistently, even when they don't feel like it. Christians who are serious about their relationship with God train themselves, too. But rather than pump iron or run laps, they train by practicing the spiritual disciplines.

Let's listen to Paul again as he shows us the difference between physical and spiritual training:

> *Train yourself* to be godly. For physical training is of some value, but godliness has value for all things, holding promise for both the present life and the life to come. This is a trustworthy saying that deserves full acceptance (and for this we labor and strive)... (1 Timothy 4:7-10, emphasis added).

If this sounds like *work* to you...you're right.

Christians often misunderstand the Bible's teaching about sanctification. Some confuse it with justification—a terrible mistake! They have this nagging sense that only those who pray enough, read the Bible enough, and do enough "good works" are really right with God. On the other extreme are those who don't feel obligated to do anything. As long as they don't commit any *major* sins, they think they can coast into heaven while doing pretty much whatever they please.

Digging deeper:
According to Philippians
2:12-13, who is
involved in the work of
sanctification? (This
one's a little tricky!)

Neither of these extremes is biblical. Our efforts don't make us any more acceptable to God—he loves us no matter how we perform. But he *does* tell us to "work out your salvation" (Philippians 2:12). Though it doesn't earn God's acceptance, discipline has a major impact on the rate at which we grow.

It's like the difference between a piano student who practices once a month and a student who practices once a day. The teacher may love them both the same...but who do you think will do better at the recital?

A lack of discipline keeps people from living up to their potential. You may have the raw talent to play college sports. But it will never happen if you sit around waiting for the phone calls from college scouts to come pouring in. Only hard work, diligent practice, and unselfish choices will. And even then you may not get any calls. But you will have developed character in the process.

> ❝ It is a clever 'wile' of Satan to tempt men to think that they cannot *do* what God requires because they do not *feel* like doing it, or that they must *do* what they feel like doing and cannot help themselves.[4] ❞
>
> —**Jay Adams**

Our teens Josh and Jaime have made 1 Timothy 4:12 one of their favorite verses: "Don't let anyone look down on you because you are young, but set an example for the believers in speech, in life, in love, in faith, and in purity." As we've discussed this verse with them over the years, we've tried to inspire them to set an example for their peers, rather than yield to the pressure to "fit in" through compromise. Yet we've also pointed out what Paul told Timothy just three verses later: "Take pains with these things; be *absorbed* in them, so that your progress may be evident to all" (1 Timothy 4:15, NAS).

Again, it's not enough to want to become more like Jesus. You have your work cut out for you. God expects you to be making progress. And progress only comes to those who "take pains" and are "absorbed" with becoming Christ-like.

Approaching your sanctification this way doesn't mean it's all up to *you* now. God is the only one who could save you, and he's the only one who can sanctify you. But it's time to grow up. To start taking some responsibility for yourself spiritually. To "stop thinking like children...but in your thinking be adults" (1 Corinthians 14:20). It's time to get serious about pursuing a holy life.

3 *Pop Quiz!* These last few paragraphs have been *very* important. To make sure you got the most out of them, take the following True/False quiz.

(Answers printed upside down at bottom of page.)

❏ If you don't read the Bible enough,   T   F
God won't accept you.

❏ You are justified by Christ, but sanctified   T   F
by your good works.

❏ Your efforts speed up the process   T   F
of Christian growth.

❏ As long as you *want* to be holy, God is   T   F
satisfied with you.

❏ You have some responsibility for growing   T   F
in godliness.

So what are some of the spiritual disciplines that will help you stop thinking and acting like a child and take some responsibility for your growth in God? You'll find several over the next few pages. The ones we've listed may surprise you—they aren't typically thought of as spiritual disciplines. But from our experience, these are the areas where teens need the most training in order to perform well under pressure.

Discipline #1: Speech

In the years we've been involved in teen ministry, we have seen two main threats to the health of any youth group. Dating is the first. When it's not breeding jealousy and competition, it's distracting teens from their passion for Christ. The second is gossip.

As we noted in Study Five, teens love to talk. And their favorite topic of conversation seems to be one another. Who likes whom. Who is struggling in what area. Who has overly strict parents. Who was seen at the mall wearing what. Who is overweight or wears too much makeup. Who talks too much or too loud.

You've been involved in these conversations.

"Have you heard…? Can you believe what she was wearing…? Keep this to yourself, but…."

Answers: F, F, T, F, T

128

Think about Psalm 39:1 and Proverbs 17:28. If you want to be wise, buy yourself a muzzle!

God knows it's tempting to gossip. Proverbs 18:8 describes gossiping words as "choice morsels"—tasty little tidbits that make us want more. What's true of Lay's potato chips is true of gossip: "bet ya can't eat just one." Our ears prick up when we hear "inside" information. And when we make others look bad, we look good in comparison.

Most Christian teens know it's wrong to make remarks such as, "She's so disgusting" or "He's such a jerk." But gossip is sneaky. It can come out in several different ways:

> 66 It is time for us Christians to face up to our responsibility for holiness. Too often we say we are 'defeated' by this or that sin. No, we are not defeated; we are simply disobedient.[5]
>
> 99
>
> —Jerry Bridges

Flattery. Saying negative things behind someone's back but positive, kind things in person.

Criticism. Looking for faults; thinking you have a "gift of discernment" when in fact you're just critical; being quick to see—and talk about—problems in others.

Slander. Exaggerating facts or putting your "slant" on what happened in order to hurt someone's reputation.

Innuendo. Communicating only part of the truth (for example, saying "I heard Susan was put on restriction last week" even though you know her parents later changed their decision); nonverbal communication such as raising your eyebrows, sighing, or rolling your eyes when someone's name is mentioned.

Backbiting. Allowing a person to believe you are a loving, loyal friend when you are actually communicating hurtful or negative things about him or her to others.

Digging deeper: The following verses can help you get a handle on your speech: Psalm 12:2, 31:13, 34:13, 141:3; Proverbs 10:18, 13:3.

You may not be the type who talks about others this way. That's great. But before you skip to the next section, ask yourself this: What do you do when *others* start to gossip? Do you walk away? Plug your ears? Tell those who are talking that they should be quiet? Most teens just listen. And letting gossip come in through your ears is just as sinful as letting it come out of your mouth.

Teens, please don't do this. Ask God to give you a conviction about the danger of gossip—in your life and in the lives of others.

Discipline #2: Self-Control

Self-control is one of the clearest signs that someone is an authentic Christian (Galatians 5:22). Those who have it are able to say "no" to selfish desires or impulses that threaten their conformity to Jesus Christ. Those who don't are often at the mercy of these desires. They have problems with things such as anger, overeating, or recurring mood swings. (By the way, most would say these things are normal and acceptable in the teen years. If you can find that anywhere in the Bible, we'd like to know about it!)

Teens face a critical need for self-control in three main areas:

Appetites. Sorry, parents—we're not going to tell your teens they have to stop eating pizza (though that might cut your food expenses in half!). Some teens need to learn to control their eating, but we're more concerned about other appetites, such as lust (uncontrolled sexual attraction), or an excessive desire for entertainment and leisure (leading to laziness, hyperactivity, and the attitude that certain activities—like church meetings or family conversations around the table—are "boring"). Teens are also vulnerable to materialism (never being content with what their parents can provide, always wanting the "newest" things).

Moods and emotions. Teens go through incredible changes physically and hormonally which can tempt them to worry about externals. (Am I too fat? Too skinny? Liked by my friends? Good enough to make the football team?) If you're like most teens, it's not uncommon for you to experience pretty dramatic mood swings. One minute you're in the depths of despair—the next you're feeling great about life.

> **❝** There are certain things we must not pray about—moods, for instance. Moods never go by praying, moods go by kicking....We have to take ourselves by the scruff of the neck and shake ourselves, and we will find that we can do what we said we could not.[6] **❞**
>
> **—Oswald Chambers**

But your hormones aren't really the problem. In general, bad moods are selfish reactions to the fact that things just aren't going your way. Like a bad hair day. A disappointing test score. No money for a new pair of shoes. You won't change things by blaming them all on hormones. Submit your feelings to God...then kick that self-centered mood out the door!

Temper tantrums, harshness, romantic infatuation, or a recurring sour disposition are some of the signs that indicate you lack emotional self-control. You may not even be aware that you're acting this way. If your parents or someone else point these out to you, trust them. They can see the signs a lot better than you can.

Think about Proverbs 15:12. Is it possible you have "blind spots" that only others can see?

130

4 At some point during the next few days, ask your parent(s) the following question (then write their answer in the space below): *"In what ways do you see me get out of control?"*

Speech. Gossip isn't the only way you can grieve God with your speech. The Bible gives us some strong warnings about how we use our tongues. Look at these verses:

> When we put bits into the mouths of horses to make them obey us, we can turn the whole animal. Or take ships as an example. Although they are so large and are driven by strong winds, they are steered by a very small rudder wherever the pilot wants to go. Likewise the tongue is a small part of the body, but it makes great boasts. Consider what a great forest is set on fire by a small spark. The tongue also is a fire, a *world of evil among the parts of the body*. It corrupts the whole person, sets the whole course of his life on fire, and is itself set on fire by hell (James 3:3-6, emphasis added).
>
> If anyone considers himself religious and yet does not keep a tight rein on his tongue, he deceives himself and his religion is worthless (James 1:26).

God obviously has an opinion on speech! As teens and parents, we must act on these words. We may love God and be respected in our churches, but if we don't have control of our tongues, the Bible says we have a serious problem.

Taming our tongues is the most difficult of the disciplines. Rather than find selfish fulfillment by speaking in ways that hurt others, we must learn to:

■ Speak the truth in love (Ephesians 4:15)
■ Refrain from gossip (Proverbs 10:18)
■ Avoid speaking against another (James 4:11)
■ Stay away from rude joking (Ephesians 5:4)
■ Refrain from sarcasm (Proverbs 26:24-25)
■ Use our speech to encourage, comfort, and build up others (Proverbs 16:24)

Digging deeper: For some other important Bible passages regarding speech, see Proverbs 21:23, 22:11; Isaiah 50:4; 1 Corinthians 14:26; Ephesians 4:29.

Discipline #3: Personal Pursuit Of God

The spiritual disciplines you'll find in this section are more familiar than speech and self-control, but they are definitely worth reviewing. As teens, you've come into a season of life when Mom and Dad are no longer able to "carry" you spiritually. What we mean is this: the Bible stories and videos and cute little music tapes they used to provide for you won't do it anymore. You're becoming a young man or young woman. It's time to start going to God on your own.

Today's teens are a busy generation. There's school. Homework. After-school clubs. *Very* important telephone conversations with friends. Fingernail polish to apply. Research at the library. Video games and favorite TV shows. Soccer practice. Haircuts. Youth meetings. With so much going on, finding time for Bible reading or prayer may seem next to impossible.

> 〟 Do we look on 'religious training' as something for toddlers but not for preteens and teens? We shy away long before our children are formed in solid, mature Christian commitment. During these years, training our children in personal prayer and scripture study, in family worship, in righteousness and obedience and willing service, are vitally important.[7] 〞
>
> **—John Blattner**

And you wonder why your walk with the Lord has become dry and mechanical.

Who is your closest friend? How did you get to be so close? By spending time getting to know each other. Do you get together or talk only two or three times a month? Probably not—unless you have a pretty loose definition of friendship.

No. You talk frequently. Share common interests. Enjoy just being together—even for no reason. You understand each other and look forward to seeing one another. The two of you talk about things you wouldn't discuss with just anybody.

If you're a Christian, Jesus wants to have this kind of relationship with you. In Revelation 3:20 he says: "Here I am! I stand at the door and knock. If anyone hears my voice and opens the door, I will come in and eat with [get to know] him, and he with me." This verse has typically been used to communicate God's heart for the unsaved. But this wasn't spoken to non-Christians. Jesus is talking to the *church*. He is expressing his longing for a relationship with *you*!

5 It's 7:30 on a Saturday morning, and you're trying to come out of a deep sleep. Suddenly you realize somebody is tapping on your window...it's your best friend! What would you say?

❏ "Get lost! I'm trying to get some sleep."

❏ "What's the deal? I talked to you just last month."

❏ "Go away and come back later."

❏ "Sorry—I'm just not in the mood to get together today."

❏ "Good to see ya! Come on in!"

You're not really following Jesus if you simply accept the free gift of salvation and then go on with your life—that is, giving all your time to your interests and hobbies and friends. To grow as a Christian you must work at deepening your relationship with the Lord. British church leader Arthur Wallis said it this way: "If you're not hungry, you're not healthy." (It's true. Who wants to eat when you have a stomach flu or a bad cold?) In the same way, if you're not spiritually hungry—if you push God to the side of your plate the way you would liver or asparagus—then you're not spiritually healthy.

Spiritually healthy teens are those who hunger for God.

Teens, your parents have no problem knowing when you're hungry. (When Josh and Jaime invite their friends over, sometimes it looks like a bulldozer has plowed through our kitchen!) But how can you tell if you are *spiritually* hungry? Here are three unmistakable clues:

Digging deeper: The Bible often stresses the importance of these spiritual disciplines: **Prayer** (Matthew 6:6, 26:41; Mark 11:24; Luke 18:1; Ephesians 6:18), **Bible reading** (Psalm 119:11, 119:103; Ephesians 6:17; Colossians 3:16), **Worship** (1 Chronicles 16:29; Psalm 27:4, 95:6, 96:9), **Becoming like Christ** (Romans 8:29; 2 Corinthians 3:18; 2 Peter 1:4; 1 John 3:9-10)

■ You have regular devotional times—including prayer and Bible reading.

■ You're not self-conscious in worship. Both in public meetings and private worship you freely express your love for God.

■ You're growing in Christ-like character. Those who spend consistent time in God's presence naturally become like him.

For the spiritually hungry Christian, discipline takes on a whole new meaning. It's not a list of "have tos" but of "want tos." Are you tired of an up-and-down walk with God? Are you sick of giving in to the temptation of sin? Do

Think about 1 Corinthians 15:9-10. Once he was saved, did Paul sit back and relax? Why or why not?

you want to know God as your close Friend and be used by him in the lives of others? Then get to know him. Run after him. Give up the junk food and sink your teeth into the Bread of Life.

You *make* time for what is most important. Make time for Jesus.

"Go To Your Right"

Our son Josh is left-handed. When he started playing organized basketball at age 11 he naturally used his left hand. He dribbled and shot left-handed. And he always drove to his left toward the basket.

One summer he had the opportunity to get some one-on-one time with an assistant college coach. "Josh," he said, "you've got some talent. But you'll never get anywhere in basketball unless you learn to go to your right."

During the following months Josh practiced with his left hand behind his back. He made himself dribble and shoot right-handed. It was frustrating. He missed a lot of shots and dribbled out of bounds. He wanted to give up and go to his left.

> 66 Most of us are very aware of our physical appetites...But our spiritual appetites are less demanding. My spirit doesn't rumble and growl the way my stomach does when empty...If your hunger has subsided, it is imperative that you seek God's diagnosis and make whatever changes are necessary—no matter how drastic. Your condition requires immediate care.[8] 99
>
> —C.J. Mahaney

But he persevered. And it paid off. The next year several of his teammates couldn't tell which hand was his strongest.

Teens, you'll never get anywhere in your walk with God if you stick to what comes "naturally." It's natural to skip your devotional time. Sleep in. Hit the snooze button just once more. Put off reading the Bible or studying what it says about a particular issue you're facing. Let your mind wander while the pastor is teaching. Hold back in your worship out of a concern that others are watching.

You've got to learn to *go to your right*. Do what's hard or awkward at times. Get up to have your devotional time when you're tired. Persevere when the things you read in the Bible don't make a lot of sense. Worship from your heart even when you don't necessarily feel like it.

Discipline is for those who are *serious* about God. That's why wannabes need not apply. ∎

QUESTIONS FOR PARENTS

1. What do your spiritual workouts include on a weekly basis?

2. Do you understand the difference between justification and sanctification? (Hint: One is complete, one is ongoing.)

3. What role does human effort play in the process of sanctification?

4. Would your teen describe you as self-controlled?

QUESTIONS FOR TEENS

1. According to the authors, why do teens "choke" under pressure? (Page 123)

2. How long does it take a Christian to become sanctified?

3. At what age do you think a young person should get serious about God?

4. What threatens to keep you from living up to your potential in Christ? (Page 127)

FACE TO FACE

1. How can you be close friends with an invisible God?

2. What motivated Paul to work so hard at living a godly life? (See Colossians 1:29 and 1 Corinthians 15:9-10)

3. In what current areas of your life do you need spiritual discipline?

4. If people lose their appetite for God, how can they get it back?

RECOMMENDED READING

John Loftness and C.J. Mahaney, *Disciplined For Life* (Gaithersburg, MD: People of Destiny International, 1992)

Robin Boisvert and C.J. Mahaney, *This Great Salvation* (Gaithersburg, MD: People of Destiny International, 1992)

Sinclair B. Ferguson, *The Christian Life* (Carlisle, PA: The Banner of Truth Trust, 1981)

R. Kent Hughes, *Disciplines of a Godly Man* (Wheaton, IL: Crossway Books, 1991)

Benny and Sheree Phillips, *Raising Kids Who Hunger For God* (Terrytown, NY: Chosen Books/Fleming Revell, 1991) Also available in audio-cassette and video series from CDR Communications, 1-800-729-2237.

Answer to Warm-Up
(from page 121): In any given year, 3,150,000 will buy a Champion jersey (that's 1 in 7); 13,408 will play NCAA ball (1 in 1,529); and only 54 will be drafted by the NBA (1 in 379,630). It takes a lot more than fashion to play with the big boys! (Thanks to Karen Grabius of Champion Products; Shirley Combs of the NCAA; and Terri Washington of the NBA.)

FRIENDS OR FOES?

BIBLE STUDY Ephesians 4:31-32

WARM-UP What has the biggest root system in the world?

A. The California redwood tree

B. Common crabgrass

C. The fungus *Armillaria ostoyae*

D. Your bottom left wisdom tooth

E. Human selfishness

(See page 150 for answer)

PERSONAL STUDY We'll call him Chad. He showed up on our doorstep in tears after another conflict with his mom. We were aware the situation was tense, but we didn't realize things had gotten that bad.

I (Sheree) spent the next two hours with Chad. Crying with him. Asking questions. Without letting him say hateful things about his parents, I listened as he voiced his anger and frustration...mostly with himself.

"Mrs. Phillips, what's wrong with me? With us? They don't trust me. And I get so angry at them. I'm almost an adult, but I feel like I'm still being treated like a little kid. I'm so tired of hearing how Christian families are supposed to be and then seeing what happens at our house. Tonight I shook my fist in my mom's face. Can you believe it? I was so mad I just had to leave. What am I gonna do?"

You need to understand something. Chad and his parents are Christians. They are actively involved in a church. Chad's dad is a kind, hard-working man. And his mom is a devoted mother. But their experience is not the rare exception. Far from it. As we've led seminars in various parts of the country, we've met family after family like

Chad's. And yet to see them in public, you would never guess what conflicts occur behind the closed doors of their homes.

Instead of being friends, they've become foes.

Chad didn't come to our house looking for a sympathetic, "you poor, mistreated kid with overprotective parents" response. He knew us better than that. And he left aware of what needed to change in *him*, not in his parents. Still, the problem was clearly two-sided.

Think about Malachi 4:6. What does this last verse of the Old Testament reveal about God's plan for families?

After speaking on the phone several times with his parents, we decided a group discussion would be the best solution. So a few days later we met to talk about the issues with the three of them.

Naturally, they had a number of specific questions. Should Chad be allowed to spend time with a non-Christian (but nice) girl he had recently met? Was or wasn't he being honest about his real feelings for her? Had he been out one hour or two hours during a recent visit to a friend's house? Weren't the parents being too strict and overly protective?

It didn't take long to see that giving our opinions on specific incidents wouldn't solve anything. As with most families, the root problem wasn't disagreements over what Chad should and shouldn't be allowed to do. It was a breakdown in the **relationship** between two parents and their teen.

So instead of getting bogged down in details, we focused on things like fear. Bitterness. Misconceptions about parental authority. Unforgiveness for past failures or mistakes. Anger. Pride. Disappointment. Unmet expectations and unfulfilled dreams. Sadness on both sides about the condition of the relationship. Guilt. A sense of hopelessness that things between them would ever get better.

> ❝ Rules only, without relationship, equals rebellion. Relationship only, without rules, equals chaos.[1] ❞
>
> —Anonymous

During the course of the evening Chad's parents were forced to listen to their son. They found out things about him they didn't know. And Chad heard his parents communicate their concerns and fears in a way he hadn't heard before.

We wish we could say all their problems were solved in our living room that night. But they weren't. Problems that take years to develop don't go away in a few hours. Yet, because of their courage to recognize *root causes* rather than be preoccupied with outward symptoms, Chad and his parents took a big step that evening toward renewing their relationship.

Going After The Roots

Our daughter Jaime was five years old when we moved into our home. Because it had been unkept for several years, the backyard was full of dandelions.

"Mommy, look at all the pretty flowers in the yard!" she exclaimed when she saw them. For days Mommy proudly displayed yellow bouquets throughout the house.

That is, until Josh mowed the lawn. Jaime couldn't understand why we would want to cut down such beauty. But we were glad to get rid of the pesky weeds.

In no time, though, they were back. Jaime would pick as many as she could before it was time for the yard to be mowed again. All summer long this process continued. Pick and mow. Pick and mow. At some point it hit us: if we don't get rid of these things, the little fuzzy ones are going to blow all over our yard and make even more! It looked like the next summer was going to be a thrilling one for Jaime with us up to our knees in weeds.

That's when we went to the garden store and bought weed killer. (We couldn't bear to tell Jaime what it was.) We faithfully applied it. Re-applied it. And even dug up parts of the yard to yank up the roots of the larger weeds.

Our summer of dandelions reminded us of an important lesson: don't think you're getting rid of something just because you "mow" it from sight. You can be sure it will come back—and sometimes even stronger and *more* visible.

---

1 All the problems listed below are symptoms of a sick parent/teen relationship, but can you tell the roots from the fruits? Circle the ones you consider root causes.

(Answers printed upside down at bottom of next page.)

Slamming doors	Arguing	Refusing to forgive
Pride	Overreacting	Despair
Lying	Selfishness	Complaining
Bitterness	Criticizing	Unwillingness to talk

As Christians, we can't just look at externals. It's too easy to deceive ourselves into thinking that because we've dealt with the symptoms, the problem is cured. Take Chad, for example. He certainly needs to stop yelling at his parents. But his real problem goes much deeper. Yelling is just an expression of his selfishness and pride. He might manage to get control of his tongue, but unless he and his parents deal with the root, these character weaknesses will pop up somewhere else.

Digging deeper: The Pharisees criticized Jesus' disciples for not washing their hands. According to Jesus, was this the real issue? (See Matthew 15:1-2, 16-20)

Or here's another example. Consider the homeowner who, after finding an inch of water in his basement, plugs a large hole in a ceiling pipe. He mops up the basement and thinks the problem is solved. But later that day he notices more water on the floor. Looking up, he finds water dripping from several smaller holes in the pipe—holes he hadn't noticed earlier because he assumed the bigger hole had caused all the damage.

We all tend to focus on the big holes in our lives and the lives of others. "Big" things like angry outbursts. Blatant selfishness. Obviously evil influences like pornographic movies or rock lyrics promoting suicide. As long as we avoid these things—or plug them up when we see them—we think we'll be okay.

Like the dandelions, however, they may "disappear" for awhile. But they'll be back.

Grace Is For Growth

When we start talking like this, some people say, "Wait a minute. Aren't you overreacting a little? After all, God's grace is sufficient for us as Christians. We just need to relax and lighten up, *especially* with our teens!"

Comments like this reveal an ignorance of the Bible's teaching. God's grace—his unmerited acceptance and favor—isn't given to help us "relax" or make us lazy when dealing with sin. Grace motivates us to grow. To work hard. To participate in the sanctification process. Pastor and author John Piper says it well: "Grace is not simply leniency when we have sinned. Grace is the enabling gift of God not to sin. Grace is power, not just pardon."[2]

The more you understand grace, the less content you will be simply to "mow down" or "plug up" the outward things. Once you've understood the price Jesus paid for your sin and had your eyes opened to see how amazing grace really is, you'll want to pursue holiness no matter how much it costs you.

Think about Titus 2:11-12. What does the grace of God teach us to do?

Those who accurately understand God's grace don't lower their standards. You won't hear them say, "God understands my weaknesses" or "We all make mistakes." Just the opposite! Grace gives them both the desire and ability to live up to God's high standards.

Consider what Jesus taught about murder and adultery in the fifth chapter of Matthew (see verses 21-22, 27-28). If he had seen grace as a cover-up for sin, he would have said, "Don't worry—I accept you just as you are. I'd appreciate it if you didn't do these things, but I understand you're human. So if you murder someone or commit adultery, don't go on a guilt trip. You're not under the law anymore. You're under grace! And I'll gladly forgive you."

Jesus did something his followers probably weren't expecting. He not only condemned murder and adultery (the externals) but he went much further. He said that hatred and lust—the internal *roots* of murder and adultery—were equally wrong.

> ❝ If you consider yourselves to have died in his death, and risen to a new way of life in his resurrection, sin will dominate you no more. You now live under a regime of grace, and grace does not stimulate sin, as law does; grace liberates from sin and enables you to triumph over it.³ ❞
>
> **—F.F. Bruce**

Do you see our point? Grace doesn't lower the standard—it *raises* it!

You may be wondering how this discussion of grace relates to parents and teens. It couldn't be more relevant. Why? Because parents and teens who properly understand God's grace are eager to expose, confess, and repent of deeply-rooted sins. They value their relationship more than their need to be "right." They are humble enough to admit when they are wrong. And they are always willing to raise the standard in their home—a *biblical* standard that pleases God, whether or not every family member agrees.

Do these kinds of people really exist? Yes. You may know some. We do.

Take 16-year-old Andy—he and his parents care enough about their relationship to discuss it with us regularly. Cry over it. Acknowledge sin and ask for forgiveness from each other.

Our friends, Larry and Doris—who regularly ask for input and observations about their teenage children or their own parenting skills.

Phyllis—a single mom in our church who recently asked the parents of her son's friend for their feedback. She wanted to know if they observed any character flaws in him, wrong attitudes, or anything that might hinder him from maturing in the Lord.

Patsy—a pastor's wife who could easily be concerned with protecting her reputation, but instead willingly admits her weaknesses as a parent. In order to grow, she often asks other moms for their advice and suggestions.

Jessica—a 15-year-old who ended a weekend with our family by asking if we saw any areas where she could improve as a Christian.

Do these people suffer under some legalistic pressure to have others approve of them? We don't think so. These parents and teens just take their walk with God seriously. They are humble and teachable. And grace makes them eager to overcome any obstacles that lie in their way.

> ❝ So very many of the heartaches in the parent-teen relationship could be avoided if only parents can apply humility, patience, understanding, prayer, and consistency to the task.[4] ❞
>
> —**Jay Kesler**

We can learn something from their example. It's time to stop making excuses for immaturity and sin. Our relationship as parents and teens is at risk. Unless we deal with sinful actions and attitudes, we're going to hurt the people we love most.

---

2 When you need loving (but firm) feedback on your relationship as parent and teen, who could you ask?

In the following sections, we've listed the offenses that so often damage the relationship between parents and teens. But you'll have to use this information wisely. Do *not* read these lists looking for proof that your parent(s) or your teen is the cause of all the trouble. The Bible teaches us to take responsibility for our *own* sin or weaknesses, rather than looking for reasons to blame others (see Matthew 7:1-5).

So pause for a minute to examine your heart. Are you ready to hear what God is telling you? Will you humbly focus on first pulling the log out of your own eye? Then—and only then—should you try helping others remove their splinters.

Under The Microscope: Teens

Teen, if you are responding to your parents in any of the following ways, you've got some work ahead of you. These are sins. Minimizing or excusing them (even when your parents fail or hurt you) will only make them worse. Rather than looking only at the problems (ways you think *your parents* need to change), start letting God reveal the solutions (ways he thinks *you* need to change).

Digging deeper: Read Psalm 51:7-13. Before David showed others their faults, what was his posture before God?

Disrespectful attitudes

☐ Arguing.

☐ Challenging their decisions (especially about what you are and aren't allowed to do).

☐ Rudely interrupting.

Angry reactions or outbursts

☐ Outward things such as yelling, slamming doors, pushing/hitting, stomping around the house.

☐ Inward things like pouting, seething, hateful thoughts, or "I can't wait to get out of the house" attitudes.

Dishonesty

☐ Lying about your whereabouts or activities.

☐ Not telling the whole truth (Example: "Mom, my new friend is really nice and she even goes to church"...but only at Christmas and Easter!).

Rejecting their standards or values

☐ Disobeying or compromising your parents' standards in your activities, choice of friends, entertainment, or interaction with the opposite sex.

Peer dependence

☐ Valuing the opinions and standards of your peers more than those of your parents.

☐ Insisting on dressing and acting like your friends.

Independent attitudes and actions

Think about Proverbs 12:15. What does the Bible call someone who goes his own way?

☐ Making decisions about curfews, friends, activities, church involvement, future plans, car usage, or other things without asking your parents.

Emotional withdrawal from the family

☐ Spending less time with family and more time with friends.

☐ Interacting with your family only when you "feel like it."

☐ Retreating into your room.

> *" Satan knows well that you will make up the next generation, and therefore he employs every craft quickly and early to make you his own. I would not have you ignorant of his devices.*
>
> *You are those on whom he displays all his choicest temptations. He spreads his net with the most watchful carefulness, to entangle your hearts. He baits his traps with the sweetest morsels, to get you into his power. He displays his merchandise before your eyes with his utmost ingenuity, in order to make you buy his sugared poisons, and eat his accursed dainties. You are the grand object of his attack. May the Lord rebuke him, and deliver you out of his hands.[5]* **"**
>
> —J.C. Ryle

☐ Resenting family members when they want to spend time with you.

Disloyalty

☐ Obeying your parents to their face but disobeying or compromising when they aren't around.

Resisting input from your parents

☐ Shrugging off their advice.

☐ Telling yourself "they don't understand" or "they're out of touch."

☐ Thinking too highly of your own opinions and abilities.

☐ Listening passively to their suggestions or observations rather than actively seeking their counsel.

Teens, do you feel like you just came through the meat grinder? (There's something convicting here for everyone!) Now read the list again. And this time, ask the Holy Spirit to highlight those which have strained your relationship with your parents. If you will take responsibility for *your* sinful responses to them, God will show them their sinful responses to you.

That's what this next section is all about.

3 Before the U.S. launched Operation Desert Storm in 1992, the economy was hurting and President Bush was sinking in the polls. But immediately after American troops stormed into Iraq to stop Saddam Hussein, the president's popularity shot up. Why?

☐ U.S. citizens were hoping for World War III

☐ The soldiers enjoyed the hot desert climate

☐ TV news was suddenly a lot more interesting

☐ It's easier to fix another country's problems than to fix your own!

144

Under The Microscope: Parents

Think about Philippians 2:3-4. Parents, is this your attitude toward your teen? It should be!

Parents, you've read the list above. And you're probably hoping your teen highlighted the same sections you did. But now it's your turn. If your relationship with your teen is tense, chances are better than average that you have also contributed to the breakdown. For the sake of your family, be honest with yourself as you review these five failures common among parents:

Selfishness

☐ Resenting the unique responsibilities of parenting teens, like car-pooling, lengthy discussions, and a busier family schedule.

☐ Being inflexible with your schedule—not making time to attend their sports, school, and church activities or to listen when they want to discuss things that seem unimportant to you.

☐ Expecting or requiring teens to free up your time by caring extensively for younger siblings. This can be doubly harmful by depriving younger children of needed time with you.

☐ Having the attitude, "I've trained you all these years, now I deserve to reap some benefits!"

> 66 Communication is more like ketchup than milk. You can't just turn the bottle upside down and have it come out. You've got to wait, prod it a little, and wait some more. Good communication requires a proper mood, a proper setting, careful preparation, good rapport, and good timing.[6] 99
>
> —Jay Kesler

Pride or embarrassment

☐ Assuming everything is fine in your relationship with your teen without asking for his or her assessment.

☐ Resenting your teen's behavior or lack of spirituality because it reflects negatively on *you*.

☐ Taking "credit" when your teen is doing well.

☐ Projecting guilt when your teen disappoints you, either verbally (anger, criticism, threats) or nonverbally (facial expressions, body language, avoiding eye contact).

☐ Making self-righteous comparisons: "I never acted this way toward my parents...what's wrong with you?"

☐ Minimizing your teen's sinful actions or attitudes as "no big deal" when you instinctively know they are serious problems.

□ Not admitting personal failure or weakness to your teen.

□ Hiding your family's problems from others.

Digging deeper: Read 1 Corinthians 13:4-8. How does love act when a relationship is under pressure?

Emotional withdrawal during difficulties

□ "Punishing" your teen with silence.

□ Withholding affection, time, or encouragement because your teen "doesn't deserve it."

□ Not taking initiative in the relationship because he or she has hurt you personally.

□ Harboring resentment or unforgiveness.

□ Subtly trying to make your teen feel bad for hurting, disappointing, or disobeying you.

Hypocrisy

□ Expecting more from your teen than you expect from yourself.

□ Pointing out problems in his or her life without recognizing or admitting your struggles in the same areas.

□ Expecting your teen to accept *you* in ways you're unwilling to accept him or her.

□ Acting one way for others and another way when only family is around.

Lack of grace and acceptance

□ Expressing your encouragement, warmth, and love according to how well your teen *does* rather than who your teen *is*.

□ Criticizing your teen's flaws and weaknesses more than you affirm his or her qualities and strengths.

□ Using guilt or anger to motivate your teen (James 1:20).

□ Blaming your teen for character deficiencies you failed to address when he or she was younger.

Think about Romans 15:7. When you find it hard to accept others, remember: God accepted you!

It's no accident, parents, that our list is longer. Raising teens isn't easy. And it's hard not to take it personally when the child you've poured your life into disappoints you. Like the first time he sighs or rolls his eyes at you. Lies to you. Accuses you of "not understanding" or tells you she feels you're picking on her. Prefers to spend the evening with a friend rather than you.

But for a few Spirit-led moments, take your eyes off your teen. Allow God to show you any ways *you* have contributed to the relational breakdown. And then humbly ask for his forgiveness.

Legendary football coach Vince Lombardi was right on the money when he said, "No pain, no gain." It's true in football. And it's no less true in relationships. Especially during the teenage years.

---

4 As you review the preceding list, pick the one statement that convicted you most and write it below.

What will it take for you to change?

Working Toward Change

If after reading through these lists you're hearing nothing but "job well done" from the Holy Spirit, be encouraged! And make a mental note to review them from time to time to make sure you're still on course. On the other hand, if you're feeling neck-deep in mud right about now, don't worry. (We've been in that pit ourselves.) There is a way out. God won't leave you there.

It's not enough to feel bad about sin, or even to feel convicted. What you—and God—desire is change! Putting off the old and putting on the new, as Paul says in Ephesians 4:22-24.

> **❝** They are wise parents who do not make light of those matters which their teenagers consider important. Whether the problem is a low test grade...or a runaway complexion, if it matters to our teens, then it should matter to us. Privileged is the mother or father who is trusted as a sounding board and confidant.[7] **❞**
>
> **—Dr. Robert Laurent**

As we saw in Study Eight, your relationship as parents and teen won't grow simply because you hope for it. It will grow because you work for it. Here's how.

First, resist the temptation to feel rejected by God for your failures or weaknesses. Conviction of sin is a priceless gift from God. Thank him for keeping your heart soft enough to hear his gentle corrections.

TEN QUESTIONS FOR PARENTS

1. Do I enjoy spending one-on-one time with my teen?

2. Does my teen seem to enjoy spending one-on-one time with me?

3. Do I regularly look for opportunities to be with my teen? Or would I rather spend time with my peers?

4. How much time is my teen spending with peers? Am I comfortable with that amount of time? Does time with friends seem to interfere with the time my teen spends with our family?

5. Do my teen and I talk on a regular basis? What do we most often discuss?

6. The following words describe me when I am giving correction to my teen (underline your choices): harsh; irritable; loving; critical; firm; sincere; clear; frustrated; angry; accepting.

7. The following words describe my teen when he/she is receiving correction from me (underline your choices): argumentative; not attentive; humble; gracious; confused; feeling misunderstood; angry; accepting; responsive; defensive.

8. During difficult or awkward moments/conversations, do I feel my teen's acceptance and love? Does he/she feel these things from me?

9. Over the past year, has our relationship deepened? Why or why not?

10. Have I embraced my God-given responsibility to impart to my teen convictions in his/her personal relationship with the Lord; vision for the church; way of relating to the opposite sex; work ethic; and attitudes toward work and authority?

Second, don't deceive yourself by thinking your life was fine until a couple of nosy authors (we won't mention any names!) started meddling in your affairs. Reading this material didn't *create* problems—it just made them more clear in your mind.

Third, rather than getting overwhelmed by all the work ahead of you, focus on the goal. Proverbs 23:7 talks about "the kind of man who is always thinking about the cost" of things. There are plenty of costs involved if you want God's best for your family. But focusing on them will only discourage and exhaust you. Fix your eyes on the prize: a relationship between parents and teens that will glorify God and launch the next generation into fruitful service.

Think about Hebrews 12:2. What encouraged Jesus to endure the overwhelming agony of the cross?

TEN QUESTIONS FOR TEENS

1. Do I enjoy spending one-on-one time with my parents?

2. Do my parents seem to enjoy spending one-on-one time with me?

3. Do I regularly look for opportunities to be with my parents? Or would I rather spend time with my peers?

4. Do my parents and I talk on a regular basis? What do we most often discuss?

5. Do I confide in my parents about personal issues? Am I honest with them about struggles, temptations, fears, insecurities? When was the last time we had this kind of discussion?

6. The following words describe my parents when they are giving me correction (underline your choices): harsh; irritable; loving; critical; firm; sincere; clear; frustrated; angry; accepting.

7. The following words describe me when receiving correction from my parents (underline your choices): argumentative; not attentive; humble; gracious; confused; feeling misunderstood; angry; accepting; responsive; defensive.

8. During difficult or awkward moments/conversations, do I feel my parents' acceptance and love? Do they feel these things from me?

9. Over the past year, has our relationship deepened? Why or why not?

10. Am I developing my own biblical convictions in areas where my parents have sought to train me, including my relationship with the Lord; vision for the church; way of relating to the opposite sex; work ethic; and attitudes toward authority?

Finally, deal radically with the sinful responses God has shown you. **Repent** specifically and thoroughly to God and to any family member you have hurt. **Ask for forgiveness** of one another. **Determine to change** by seeking help from God and others. (We recommend that you confess your failures to a close friend or pastor. Listen closely to their input, and ask them to follow up with you in the future.) Practice saying **"I was wrong"** the next time you blow it. In other words, clean your slate of all offenses…and keep it that way.

And when you hit a wall of disagreement, do what Chad and his parents did. Ask for help. It won't be easy, but isn't your relationship worth it? ■

QUESTIONS FOR PARENTS

1. If you could raise your child all over again, what would you do differently (if anything)?

2. Have you been content merely to plug the largest holes in your relationship with your teen? (See page 140)

3. If your teen got arrested for drunken driving, which would you feel more strongly: personal embarrassment or concern for your child?

4. How does our heavenly Father treat us when we fail to meet his expectations?

5. Does your relationship with your teen need outside help?

QUESTIONS FOR TEENS

1. In what ways could your relationship with your parents improve?

2. Can you trust God to deal with your parents about their shortcomings as you deal with your own?

3. Did this study help you identify any root problems in your life? If so, what were they?

4. Why do so many teens drift away from their parents?

FACE TO FACE

1. What are some obvious signs of a good relationship between parent and teen? (Try to think of five.)

2. Before reading this study, had you focused more on outward symptoms or root causes? (See page 139)

3. Does your relationship need "weed killer"?

4. What changes in your relationship would you like to see six months from now?

Answer to Warm-Up
(from page 137): C: The fungus *Armillaria ostoyae* (if its underground growths can be called roots). In May '92, scientists reported a network of this fungus covering some *1,500 acres* in Washington State! (Source: *Guinness Book of Records*, Peter Matthews, ed., Bantam Books, 1993) Scientists have yet to measure human selfishness... but it's a big fungus, too!

A FOUNDATION FOR THE FUTURE

BIBLE STUDY Matthew 7:24-27

WARM-UP To live in California is to live with the constant threat of earthquakes. The one that rocked Los Angeles in January '94 measured 6.6 on the scale. Though not the "Big One," it did plenty of damage. How long did it take this quake to rack up the following?

■ 57 deaths

■ 250 gas lines ruptured

■ Nine highways snapped like twigs

■ Electricity cut off for 3.1 million people

■ Local mountains raised as much as a foot

(See page 167 for answer)

PERSONAL STUDY He was handsome and athletic. Loved by everyone—from the homeless man he saw regularly on the street to the little girl he met while working as lifeguard at the local pool. In fact, he was a hometown hero of sorts. Raised in a small West Virginia town, he had become the star of the high school football team, and had received an athletic scholarship to college.

He'd also gotten a new car. And one night some friends talked him into seeing just how fast it could go.

You guessed it—the car was totaled. For over an hour, paramedics tried in vain to revive him. They just couldn't give up on the kid they had all grown to love so much.

Practically the whole town showed up for his funeral. The homeless man said, "He was my friend." The little girl from the pool sobbed. Friends and family cried and wondered how this could have happened. His older brother gave thanks that just weeks earlier he had seen him get things right between himself and God.

151

Think about Proverbs 15:21. How can teens make sure they "stay on the road" without crashing?

This 19-year-old had everything going for him. His future was bright and full of promise. Yet one foolish choice cost him his life. He'll never hear the roar of the crowd at a game again. Never get married or become a dad. Never lead a friend to Jesus Christ.

In a split second he made a costly decision. The decision to ignore the voice of his conscience and give in to his friends.

"But if he had only known what was about to happen, he would never have done it!" you say.

And you're right. Of course he wouldn't have done it. But it's not often we get warned in advance about the consequences of foolish decisions. For example:

■ When you watched that movie, you didn't realize your mind would keep playing back the worst parts of it for weeks to come.

■ How could you have known that your new friend's disrespectful attitudes toward her parents would start rubbing off on you?

■ Hey, it was supposed to be a party for a few friends at school….No one told you kids would be drinking and pairing off as couples.

Unwise decisions such as these probably won't kill you. But little by little, wrong decision after wrong decision, you'll slowly lose your spiritual life. Your family life. The life of purity and purpose God desires for you as a teen.

"Life Is Short…Play Hard"

As a young man or woman, you see your life as just beginning. You've got so much ahead of you. Getting your driver's license. Graduating from high school. Getting a job or going to college. Getting married. Having children.

Because the teen years are relatively short, the classic Reebok slogan seems to make a lot of sense: "Life is short … Play hard." In other words, have all the fun you can. Live for the moment—and don't take things too seriously. You're only young once.

Few teens realize just how short life is.

We parents, though, are beginning to sense it. It seems like only yesterday we brought our baby home from the hospital in our arms…and now we're looking up at him. We stare in the mirror and see "laugh lines" and gray hair and "love handles" on figures that were once smooth and trim. We answer questions from our kids like, "Do you really *remember* when John F. Kennedy was shot?" or "What's an eight-track stereo?" Then our parents start needing us in ways we once needed them, or we get news of a high school classmate who just died of a heart attack.

Take it from us, teens. Life is short.

The Bible said so long before Reebok. It describes our lives as a watch in the night and as a single blade of grass: "Though in the morning it springs up new, by evening it is dry and withered" (Psalm 90:6).

As teens, you don't yet realize how much your future depends on the choices you're making today. Even the little choices that seem so unimportant can have a serious impact on your life. That's why the Bible offers you this important advice:

> " Resolved, never to do anything which I would be afraid to do if it were the last hour of my life.[1] "
>
> —Jonathan Edwards

> Be careful, then, how you live—not as unwise but as wise, making the most of every opportunity, because the days are evil. Therefore do not be foolish, but understand what the Lord's will is (Ephesians 5:15-17).

1 When he was a boy, few would have seen the potential in George Washington Carver. Yet because of his faith in God, wise decisions, and determination, this former slave became one of America's outstanding scientists. Does his life story inspire you?

- Born in 1864 as a small, sickly child

- Father died; mother stolen by bandits

- At age 13, had to earn his own tuition money

- Accepted at Highland University; sold his small laundry business

- Prevented from enrolling because he was black

- Wandered the country in despair; almost gave up his dream of education, but decided to try again

- Became the first black to graduate from his college

- Invented peanut butter and many other products

- Got job offers from Thomas Edison *and* Henry Ford!

Because they're not being careful about the way they live, countless Christian teens are frittering away some of the most exciting and productive years of their lives. Unwise and selfish decisions are keeping them from "making the most of every opportunity." Instead of growing up in God, they're still in spiritual diapers.

The famous British preacher Charles Spurgeon said,

> A short life should be wisely spent. We have not enough time at our disposal to justify misspending it at all. Neither are we sure enough of life to justify procrastinating...If we were wise in heart we should see this, but mere head wisdom will not guide us aright.[2]

Teens, when you understand how short life really is, you won't have attitudes like these:

"I'm too young to think about discipline and sanctification and all that other stuff. I just want to have some fun."

Digging deeper: Some time this week, take a few minutes to read Psalm 90—especially verse 12. What do you think it means to "number our days"?

"Sure I blow it once in a while...doesn't everybody? But it's not like I'm doing anything *seriously* wrong."

"I'll deal with that bad habit or wrong attitude later... next week...or maybe at the next youth retreat."

"No, my parents and I aren't doing so hot. But we'll work it out sooner or later."

"Oh, I guess there are a couple of things my parents don't know I'm into. I'll tell them...uh...at some point."

Young people like honesty, right? Well, you're about to get it. Not just from two authors you've never met, but from a dad and mom who care deeply about kids like you.

If you choose to live as if there are a million tomorrows, then get ready to face the consequences. Like heartbreak over a lost girlfriend. Guilt about sexual sin or a secret abortion. Anger and bitterness toward your parents. Forsaking everything you've been taught by your parents for a few adolescent thrills. Living life as a counterfeit Christian who has never really been saved. Watching jealously as old friends of yours, who stayed pure and passionately devoted to God, leave you in the dust spiritually.

We don't mean to be harsh. But our hearts ache for all the teens we've seen who started out well but ended up fools. The young people who are really making their lives count for the kingdom of God are those who are refusing to live for pleasure and popularity and applause. They're living for Jesus Christ—and they recognize that *now* is the time to make their lives count for him!

Will It Pass Inspection?

Several years ago we built an addition onto our home to create an apartment for Mom (Sheree's mother). The first step was getting rid of a huge tree so that a bulldozer could come and dig the foundation. Our back yard was a mess. Mud and tree parts were everywhere! Finally it was time for the concrete. Our friends helped haul wheelbarrow after wheelbarrow load as we slowly filled the hole in our yard. The concrete was then carefully raked, smoothed, and leveled—and left for several days to dry. Throughout the whole process, inspectors came regularly to make sure every step was done just right. Sometimes they made us change or improve things. (And at times it seemed they were being awfully picky!)

> **“** Satan cares not how spiritual your intentions may be, and how holy your resolutions, so long as they are fixed for tomorrow. Oh, give no place to the devil in this matter! Tell him, 'No: Satan! It shall be today: today!'[3] **”**
>
> —J.C. Ryle

This stage of the project seemed to take forever. *If laying the foundation took this long,* we thought, *it's going to be a long time before we ever see the addition.* And yet in just a few weeks the outside was complete and the inside walls were going up.

Why did the foundation take so long? Because it's the most important part of construction. If the foundation isn't right, the building isn't safe. And once it's done, the rest goes up quickly. Before we knew it, our children were enjoying breakfast with Nannie in her new apartment.

Your foundation is equally important, teens. And you're "pouring the concrete" right now. By the lifestyle choices you make today you are building a foundation for the future. *Your* future. That's why the Bible says to "be careful" how you live during these years. Be careful to build a strong, solid foundation that will pass the Inspector's test. He has given you all you need to do a beautiful job, and he won't overlook sloppy work.

Think about Ecclesiastes 11:9. As Matthew Henry once said, "It ought to be the business of every day to prepare for our last day."

As we mentioned at the beginning of this book, today's teens are different than the "youths" of former generations—especially in their view of the future. When they were your age, your grandparents were preparing to tackle the responsibilities of adult life. But your generation is living for the moment. Hardly a thought is given to the critical decisions that lie just around the corner. You're too busy having fun.

2 In the years to come, you will face many of the following choices. Put a check in the box beside any of these you have already thought about.

❑ Areas of gifting and service in your church

❑ Career direction

❑ College (Will you go? Where? What will you study?)

❑ Who will you marry?

❑ When will you start a family?

❑ Where will you live?

Some of you are probably saying, "Hey, wait a minute! The only thing I'm thinking about right now is the math test I have to take on Tuesday. What's all this heavy talk about the future? I'm still a kid, you know."

We don't mean to make fun of you, teens, but we find this attitude amazing. You want adults to view you as mature and able to make your own decisions about things ...until the subject of the future comes up. Suddenly, you're "just a kid" again. That's one of the main conflicts of adolescence: wanting to be treated maturely without having to act responsibly. Caught between childhood and adulthood, you can't always decide which you'd rather be, can you? Some days you want to be more like an adult (especially when you feel your parents have made a bad decision). But other days it's nice being "just a kid."

Think about 1 Corinthians 13:11. What will you have to give up in order to grow up?

Of course we're not suggesting that, by age 16, all teens should have their careers mapped out and their weddings planned. What we *are* saying is that adolescence is a season for shifting gears. It's time to put the carefree attitudes of childhood behind you and start making wise plans for the future.

Don't get us wrong. We know the teenage years are a blast, and we're having fun re-living them with our teens. (Though we sure get tired a lot faster than we did the first time around!) We want our children to enjoy things like learning to drive, going on youth retreats, and spending time with friends. But we also want to prepare them for some decisions they'll be facing sooner than they realize.

In fact, that's what this whole book has been about. We can't offer any new gimmicks or gadgets to help you get ready for the future. Instead, we've tried to show you the time-tested, biblical path to maturity. As we've mentioned throughout the book, you need to:

Cultivate a strong relationship with the Lord. You can't expect to get clear guidance from God in the future if you aren't used to hearing and obeying his voice *now*. Learn how to seek him on today's smaller issues. Explore his Word. Practice prayer. Draw near to him in worship. All these will make it easier to receive his counsel concerning the bigger decisions ahead.

Have a teachable heart toward those in authority. Soon God will give you your own place of authority—in the home, in the workplace, in the church, or elsewhere. But you can't handle being *in* authority until you've learned the value of being *under* authority. Begin with your parents. Even when you don't agree with them, your attitude toward them should be respectful and humble.

Develop character. Nobody can tell you what your future holds. But we *can* tell you what you'll need to face it successfully. You'll need courage. Patience. Honesty. Spiritual passion. Diligence. Character qualities like these (and there are lots more!) will keep your life on target. Best of all, they will help you lead a life that pleases God.

> **“** There is only one relationship that matters, and that is your personal relationship to a personal Redeemer and Lord. Let everything else go, but maintain that at all costs, and God will fulfill his purpose through your life. One individual life may be of priceless value to God's purposes, and yours may be that life.[4] **”**
>
> **—Oswald Chambers**

There's another area we haven't discussed much: *practical preparations for the future*. For example, if you believe God is calling you to go to college, don't wait till your first semester to learn good study skills. Start now! (And begin putting some of your money into a savings account...college is expensive!) Also, even as a teen you can learn a lot about marriage by watching the way godly Christian couples speak with and treat one another. To get ready for a job, make the most of today's opportunities. Doing household chores or getting up at 5 a.m. to deliver papers may not be your idea of a career, but the work habits you develop will serve you well in the future.

We don't have space to go into detail, but there are plenty of good materials that can help you determine career direction, establish a budget, prioritize your schedule, and so on. Your parents can help you find these.

Straw, Sticks, And Bricks

Preparing for the future doesn't mean you have to become like this overly conscientious teen:

"Sorry, Sue, I don't think I can come over today. My day is looking pretty full. Right now I'm getting some tips on how to communicate with my future husband...How? By watching my parents figure out whose fault it was that the electric bill didn't get paid. Then I'm scheduled to spend the afternoon with Mom's friend, Mrs. Adams... yeah, she had a little girl, so she's gonna give me some pointers on taking care of a newborn baby. Then I'll be over at Dad's office, getting a crash course in computer networking and time management skills. But if I have any time left, I'll give you a call."

Digging deeper: Read Proverbs 6:6-8. What lessons could you learn from a teenage ant?

As we said, the teen years can and should be enjoyable. But not at the expense of getting ready for the future. Can you imagine what shape your body would be in if you ate nothing but cookies, candy, and ice cream? (Round!) For those who think the teen years were made only for having fun, it's time to change your diet. Vegetables may not taste as good as a Snickers bar, but you need them. Likewise, hanging out with friends and collecting CDs may be fun. But if that's your main focus as a teen, you'll never be ready to face the responsibilities waiting for you as an adult.

3 Dieticians talk about the four basic food groups: meat, dairy products, fruits/vegetables, and grains. (Some include a fifth category: chocolate!) What are four activities you see as necessary in the "diet" of a teen's life?

■

■

■

■

Do you remember the story of the three pigs? Each pig built a house. One with sticks. One with straw. The other with bricks. The first two houses went up fast. But when the big, bad wolf started huffing and puffing, they came

Digging deeper: Read
1 Corinthians 3:10-15.
According to Paul, why
must we be careful
about the way we build?

down fast, too. Those two pigs were lucky to escape with their lives. Only the third pig had taken the time to build with the right materials. And his was the only house still standing after the enemy's attack.

We've often wondered if this story was adapted from one Jesus told in Matthew 7:24-27. He talks about two men who built houses. One built his house on the rock. When bad weather came, his house stood strong. The other guy built his house on sand. (Not smart!) And you know what happened when the rains, floods, and winds came. This man was homeless.

The first guy was a wise guy—in the best sense of the word. The second was a fool.

Jesus used this story to make an important point: "Everyone who hears these words of mine and does not put them into practice is like a foolish man" (vs. 26). It's not enough to *know* what's right. Or even to *want* to do what's right. Only those who actually *do* what they've been taught are considered wise.

Whether you realize it or not, you're in the process *now* of building your future. You'll build with straw, sticks, or brick. You'll build on the rock or you'll build on sand. You'll build on a carefully constructed, frequently inspected foundation. Or you'll rush through the process only to find yourself shoveling through piles of debris when your foundation cracks under the weight of what you built.

> **" Habits of good or evil are daily strengthening in your hearts. Every day you are either getting nearer to God, or further off.[5] "**
> —J.C. Ryle

A lot of teens have good looks, athletic ability, or marketable talent. And some of these things may help you in the future. But never make them your foundation. Only fools would build their lives on materials like this. The wise build their future on the foundation of a strong relationship with God, submission to authority, and Christlike character.

And when the storms of life come, they don't budge.

God is the Inspector. One day he will judge the quality of your work to see how well you've built, and what materials you've used. He will inspect every detail of your life. And if something's cracked or rotted or out of line, it will be too late to fix it.

Because he wants you ready for that day, God has given you parents. He has given them the grace and wisdom to build and test your foundation. Even though they make mistakes—or seem picky at times, like the inspectors who "interfered" when we were building the addition on our home—trust God to work through them. Looking back, we're glad the inspectors did their job to make sure our foundation was solid. And in the years to come, you'll appreciate the high standards of character your parents are requiring of you.

Think about John 10:10. Though Satan's promises sound nice, what three goals does he have for your life?

Like the three little pigs, you also have an enemy. The Bible shows us there is one who wants to keep your generation locked up in chains of selfishness and pride. Why? Because Satan sees that God is pouring out his Spirit on this generation of young people. God is raising up young champions who can lead a generation of teens destined for greatness. *True* greatness. Not the corrupt power that comes from money or influence or physical appeal. But the pure power that comes only by modeling the nature and character of Jesus Christ (Matthew 20:26).

A Taste For The "Real Thing"

Do you want to be one of those servant-leaders God is calling out from among your generation?

Do you want to stop wasting your teen years wondering what others think of you?

Do you want to be an "impact player" for God?

Are you prepared to deal radically with those things that are keeping you from becoming mature?

Are you humble enough to seek help from God and your parents?

Not every teen who reads this book will be willing to pay the price of greatness. Some will have "ears to hear," as Jesus said. Others won't. Some of the parents and teens who started this book never made it this far. Maybe they got bored, or felt the biblical standards were too high.

But you persevered. And that tells us you just might have what it takes to rise above the crowd and stand tall for Christ in your generation.

What *will* it take? A commitment to three basic things:

First, you'll need to *gain a taste for God's kingdom*—and lose your taste for the world. In talking about this recently with our son Josh, we explained it this way. How do you know if the soda you're drinking is Coke Classic or a grocery store imitation? By drinking can after can of the counterfeit? No. By drinking the "real thing" over and over. (After years of Coke Classic, it takes only a sip to realize Mom went for the sale-priced imitation this week!)

Digging deeper: Spit out the imitation stuff… these verses will give you a taste for God's kingdom! (1 Corinthians 15:33; 2 Corinthians 6:14-18; Ephesians 4:17-24; Colossians 3:1-10)

Once you experience authentic Christianity, you're ruined. Anything else is a cheap imitation. (Not to mention the aftertaste—yuck!) Nothing this world can offer you will come anywhere close to the fulfillment of living totally for Jesus Christ.

It would be a lie to tell you that sin isn't sometimes fun. It can be—though only for a short time (Hebrews 11:25). But consistently tasting the "good stuff" (holy and pure living) sure deadens your taste for the counterfeit (compromise and worldliness). You'll learn to say "no" to sinful desires as you consistently say "yes" to God.

---

4 Can you tell the counterfeit from the "real thing"? As you look at the list below, circle the things God wants teens to focus on; put an "X" through the things that are cheap (and dangerous) imitations.

Dating	Worship
Sharing the gospel	Drugs and alcohol
Having fun	Friendship
Serving others	Being popular

The second step naturally follows. You need to be actively *involved in a local church*. We're not just talking about attendance on Sunday morning or at youth meetings. Active involvement means understanding and giving yourself to the vision of the church. Serving in meaningful and behind-the-scenes ways. Understanding that the church isn't built around meetings, but on relationships that produce maturity, discipleship, and training in Christ-like character.

Rarely does a teen have the courage to stand all alone against the raging tide of peer conformity and worldly temptations. You need friends who share your convictions, friends even more eager to obey and follow God than you are. As you interact and serve with them in the church, they will inspire and challenge you. Over time, you also can become an example to younger, less mature teens who will look to you for help.

A quick word to parents: The responsibility of raising teens may cause you to face some unexpected decisions about church involvement. Maybe you've been in the same

TEN MARKS OF A BIBLICAL CHURCH

■ Is Jesus Christ exalted as the resurrected Son of God? (Acts 2:24)

■ Is the Bible honored and taught as the authoritative guide for faith and practice? (2 Timothy 3:16-17)

■ Is there freedom and vitality in the worship? (Colossians 3:16)

■ Rather than merely attend meetings, do the people build deep, honest relationships? (Acts 2:42-47)

■ Do the leaders exercise both pastoral care and authority? (1 Peter 5:2-3)

■ Are the members motivated by commitment rather than convenience? (Acts 2:42)

■ Do leaders place more emphasis on character than on charisma? (1 Timothy 3:1-13)

■ Is there input from those gifted as apostles, prophets, evangelists, pastors and teachers? (Ephesians 4:11-15)

■ Is there an outward, evangelistic thrust to reach others with the gospel? (Matthew 28:19-20)

■ Have people's lives been positively changed through their involvement? (Romans 12:2)

church for years—since before your children were teens. You have friends in the church, and may even serve on various committees or provide some level of leadership. People depend on you and you on them. And yet, if you were totally honest, you may agree that your teen isn't growing in this environment. Maybe the youth group is more of a social club than a training ground for godly living. Or perhaps some of the things we've discussed—gossip, dating, worldliness, and so on—have infected the young people and quenched their passion for God. And you're realizing that "peer conformity" isn't just a problem in non-Christian environments. It also happens in the church.

We're not trying to criticize your church or tell you what to do. But we want to challenge you with this: *Take seriously the spiritual condition of your teen.* Do not presume he or she will turn out okay in the end. It's precisely that attitude which has created the tragedy described by Dr. Robert Laurent in his book, *Keeping Your Teen in Touch with God*:

> Over fifty percent of Christian teenagers will sit in church next Sunday morning. Within two years, seventy percent of them will have left the church, never to return…Gallup polls report that sixty-five percent of evangelical teens never read their Bibles and thirty-three percent feel that religion is out-of-date and out-of-touch.[6]

The church is essential for your teen's growth in God. If the church you attend is not spurring your teen on—or worse, if its youth are dragging your teen down—then you

Digging deeper: Read Ephesians 4:14-16. This is God's goal for the church...is it happening in yours?

must prayerfully consider making a change. To stay on the basis of misguided loyalty while your teen stumbles into worldliness could have eternal consequences.

If you sense God may be leading you elsewhere, please talk with your pastor. Share your concerns without being critical. Ask for his counsel, then pray some more before making a final decision. It's possible that God would use you (with your pastor's support and cooperation) to help make some healthy changes in the group.

(On the previous page is a list of characteristics the New Testament says should exist in a church. And in Appendix B on page 171, we offer some suggestions about what to look for in a church's youth ministry.)

Back to you, teens. To stand tall for Christ in your generation, the third step you must take is to *submit yourself afresh to your parents' authority*. God has placed you under their care. Others can supplement—but your parents' counsel, leadership, and authority is critical for your well-being.

We know it's not always as simple as it may sound. What happens if your parents give you wrong counsel? What if one or both aren't Christians? What if your mom and dad are divorced and give you conflicting opinions? These issues are simply too complex to cover without knowing the personal history of each situation. If something like this applies to you, get some input from your pastor or a trusted Christian advisor.

For most of you, however, the questions you face are much more basic. What if you don't like what your parents tell you? What if they're being too strict? What if you feel ready to start making decisions on your own, but they aren't convinced you have the maturity?

> ❝ It is extremely difficult, perhaps impossible, for someone to obey God, whom they have never seen, if they are unwilling to obey visible and tangible human authorities.[7] ❞
>
> —Fran Sciacca

You're almost finished with this book, so you know the answer we're about to give. Humble yourself. And, like Jesus, who "learned obedience from what he suffered" (Hebrews 5:8), recognize that God is much more concerned with how you respond to authority than whether the authority was perfectly executed. Focus on responding the way *you* should. In time, your humility may open the door for you to communicate something that will help your parents in areas where they are weak. (And yes, such areas exist!)

163

5 Are there certain areas in your life where you find it *especially* hard to accept your parents' authority? (Briefly describe them in the space below.)

Whether your relationship with your parents is strained or healthy, consider telling them something like this before the week's over:

> "Dad/Mom: I realize more than ever that I need your leadership in my life. I don't always make it easy for you to be a parent. But I recognize that God has placed you in authority over me. I want to commit myself to do my best to respect and obey you. I need your help to become all that God wants me to be."

Think about James 4:6. How does God treat the proud? the humble?

This may seem like a silly exercise. You may feel awkward saying it because you've never said anything like this before. But you'll know you've learned some important lessons—like the value of humility—if you go ahead and do it. Even if you and your parents are doing great, a commitment like this will only make things better.

A Final Word About Walking

Everywhere we travel we hear parents express a common concern: "I don't just want my teen to be outwardly 'Christian'—I want him/her to have a *genuine* relationship with God." That's because as parents we had our fill of empty and irrelevant religion while growing up. "Do this" and "don't do that" Christianity led many of us into compromise and sin. We want *more* for our own children.

But what will it take? How can we protect them from being among the 70% who leave the fold "never to return?" *By creating in them—and imparting to them—passion for Jesus Christ and his church.*

Scripture tells us to "train a child in the way he should go" (Proverbs 22:6). And as we saw in Study Three, this means we are to "create a thirst" in them for the things of God. But there's no way to impart passion unless we first have it ourselves.

Parents, are *you* thirsty for intimacy with God? For growth in Christ-like character? For giving your life away to others? For pure and holy living? For usefulness to God through service in his church? If your answer is yes, then you're probably influencing your teen more than you realize. If no, then your teen's lack of passion may simply be a reflection of your own.

Raising teens has exposed a lot of weakness and sin in us over the years. We've felt the fatigue of having to remind them for the third time to get started on a school project. We've spent hours talking and crying together as a couple over whether or not we're being too strict or too lenient; too involved or not involved enough. We've had to ask for their forgiveness (plenty of times!) for being harsh, selfish, or insensitive.

We have yet to meet a perfect parent. But we urge you to address those things that are hindering *your* passion for God. Ask for God's forgiveness. Pray for change. And be reconciled with your teen. In those areas where you have sinned against your children, don't just admit that you "made a mistake"—ask their forgiveness in specific detail. Not only will this exercise improve your relationship with your teen, but it will deepen *your* thirst for the things of God so that you have something passionate to impart to them.

We told you early on this book would focus on your relationship with your teen. It's been our focus as authors because it's been our passion as parents. In the midst of all our mistakes, we've always sought to protect the most precious thing we have with them: our relationship. This ending to a letter from Sheree to Jaime on her 13th birthday perhaps says it best:

> **❝** Kids want to know if the Christian faith actually works, and one way they can be shown that is to observe it working in the lives of their parents. In the end Christianity is not simply taught; it's caught. And if you ain't got it, they won't catch it.[8] **❞**
>
> —**Dawson McAllister**

Think about Matthew 5:23-24. When is the best time to restore a broken relationship?

The years ahead have so much in store for you. Fun. Laughter. Challenges. Disappointments. I want to *be there* for you through it all. I want to be the friend you can turn to. Still "the boss?" Yes. But also counselor. Companion. Confidant. Listening ear. (Let it be, Lord Jesus.)

Your teens *want* to "walk with the wise," parents. God has placed that desire in their hearts. So give them someone to follow. Show them the way to go. Share your life and love with them freely. And trust that the God who is guiding your steps will be faithful to keep their feet on the path as well. ■

QUESTIONS FOR PARENTS

1. Has your life turned out the way you thought it would when you were a teen?

2. What evidence do you see that your teen is "shifting gears" into adulthood?

3. In what practical ways are you helping your teen get ready for the future?

4. How can you be a foundation inspector without exasperating your teen (Ephesians 6:4)?

5. Are you and your teen actively involved in a church that challenges you and equips you for godliness?

QUESTIONS FOR TEENS

1. If you knew you only had one more year to live, would your life change? How?

2. One day you go to the store and notice two checkout lines: one for kids and one for adults. Which would you get in? (And you can't say, "The shortest one"!)

3. What are some of the things you're doing now to get ready for adulthood?

4. Does the world "taste" good to you? How can you tell?

5. Are you ready to *work* at being friends with your parents?

FACE TO FACE 1. What are some of the things you are looking forward to —individually and together—in the future?

2. Why do we need others to inspect our workmanship?

3. What are some of the things a young person might accomplish for God in the teenage years?

4. Why is the church essential for our growth in God?

5. The prophet Amos asked, "Do two walk together unless they have agreed to do so?" In prayer, devote these years to walking together...not just as parent and teen, but as friends.

Am I A Genuine Christian?

Benny and Sheree Phillips

During the teen years, some young people (or their parents) begin to have questions about whether or not they have been genuinely converted. These questions arise particularly in the minds of teens who:

■ Prayed to become Christians at an early age, and perhaps have no memory of the experience.

■ Are struggling with various habits, temptations, and sins they feel an authentic Christian shouldn't be dealing with.

■ Have questions about God, Christianity, or the Bible they never had when they were younger.

■ Are consistently showing a lack of Christ-like character and the fruit of the Holy Spirit (Galatians 5:22).

■ Are living a double life—doing the "good, Christian thing" when parents are around but conforming to the world when they aren't.

Nothing is more important to you as a young man or woman than to be sure of your Christian conversion. As a churched teen, you know there are serious consequences—including eternal judgment and separation from God—for those who are not true Christians. So how do you know if you're a "counterfeit Christian" or if you have been genuinely converted?

Here are some questions to ask yourself and to discuss with your parents (we've included a lot of Scripture for you to consider in answering these questions):

■ Do you believe there is absolutely nothing you can do to gain God's acceptance and favor, and that Jesus Christ is the only way to salvation? (Isaiah 53:6; John 3:16; Romans 3:9-18; 5:6, 8; Philippians 2:5-11; 2 Timothy 3:1-5; Hebrews 9:26)

■ Have you put your faith in this truth? Are you utterly convinced of it? (Acts 10:43; 16:29-31; 20:21; Ephesians 2:8-9; Hebrews 11:6)

■ Have you repented of (turned away completely from) your sin and made a "no turning back" decision to follow and obey Jesus Christ, regardless of the costs? (Luke 3:3-5; 14:25-33; Acts 17:30; 20:21)

■ When you sin, are you quick to confess it to God? (1 John 1:9)

■ Do you consistently avoid worldly, tempting situations and people except for God-ordained evangelistic endeavors? (Psalm 1:1; 26:4-5; Romans 12:2; Titus 2:11-13; 1 Peter 1:13-16; 1 John 2:15-16)

■ Is there fruit (evidence) in your life that you are a genuine Christian? (Matthew 3:8; Galatians 5:22; 2 Peter 1:5-10)

- Are you consistently pursuing God through spiritual disciplines? (See Study Eight)

- Are you unashamed of your relationship with the Lord? Are you willing to be rejected by your peers, if necessary, for the sake of the gospel? (Romans 1:16; 1 Peter 4:12-16)

- Are you experiencing the power of God in overcoming sin and sharing the gospel with others? (Acts 1:8; 2:14-41; 4:31; 6:8; Romans 8:5-11)

- Do you love the church (the people of God) and are you actively involved in a local church? (Psalm 68:6; Acts 2:42-47; 4:32; Romans 12:4-8; 1 Corinthians 12:14-27; Hebrews 10:25)

Parents and teens, take an honest look at the questions above. Carefully and prayerfully consider your answers. According to the Bible, anyone who has experienced genuine repentance and saving faith in Jesus Christ will display these characteristics.

If you realize that you've been a counterfeit Christian, make sure you're willing to make the commitments above and pray a prayer similar to this:

> *Jesus, I see now that I've never been genuinely converted. I've been living the life of a counterfeit Christian. Today I want that to change. I agree with you that I'm a sinner and that you alone can make me right with God. Please forgive me of my sin and for living independently apart from you. I need your power to say "no" to worldliness and temptation. Please give me the strength and supernatural power I need to follow and obey you for the rest of my life. Thank you for forgiving and cleansing me. Amen.*

If you prayed this prayer today, let your parents be the first to know (if they didn't share the experience with you). Then begin to tell others. Don't let the same pride and self-consciousness that caused you to live a double life until now prevent you from communicating the decision you've made to those around you. (And don't worry about what others who thought you *were* a Christian might say when they find out you just became one.)

If reading over the above list confirmed that you *are* a genuine Christian, great! We hope this exercise will energize you all the more to live a sold-out life of usefulness to God!

What Should I Expect From A Church Youth Ministry?

Benny and Sheree Phillips

Like many Christian parents, you may have joined your church when your children were very young. You feel at home there and respect the way your leaders provide biblically-based ministry to the various ages of your family members.

Or maybe you're a new Christian. Having not been involved in a church, you're not sure what to look for—especially since you now have a teenager who needs godly peers and solid, biblical teaching on some critical issues.

In either case, we hope this book has helped you understand your need to nurture the spiritual life of your child. As one element of that, it's essential that you take a close look at your church's philosophy of youth ministry.

We aren't suggesting that you be critical or fault-finding, and we know that your choice of a church depends on many factors, not just one. Yet the youth ministry has a profound effect on the lives of most churched teens. Therefore, conscientious parents will take seriously their need to examine the potential influences—both positive and negative—of a particular youth ministry on their teen.

Here are some questions to help you determine how the church's youth ministry is going to shape your child.

■ Are the primary goals of the youth ministry to train young people in Christ-like character and equip them to reach their generation with the gospel of Jesus Christ?

■ Do church leaders—and those who work with the youth in particular—display godly character (i.e. integrity, humility, purity) in their personal lives?

■ Are parents seen as those *primarily* responsible for training, equipping, and discipling their own teens? (See Deuteronomy 4:9; 6:7; 11:19; 31:13; Psalm 71:18; 78:5; Proverbs 1:8-9; 19:18; 22:6; and 1 Timothy 3:4.)

■ Are teens taught to respect, obey, and seek the counsel and training of their parents? (See Proverbs 1:8; 6:20; 20:20; 30:17; Ephesians 6:1-2; and Colossians 3:20.)

■ Are parents welcome to attend youth meetings and social functions, or would your involvement be viewed as potentially negative (i.e. squelching the teens from being themselves or having the fun they would have without parents around)?

■ Is there positive, visible fruit in the lives of the teens who are involved in the youth ministry? Are they growing in character? Learning to resist worldliness? Developing strong relationships with the Lord? (We're not suggesting that every teen must be exemplary in these ways. However, a biblically successful youth ministry leads a majority of the teens to experience the transforming power of God. Christian parents *are* ultimately responsible for their teens' growth and maturity, but the youth ministry should offer a strong supplement.)

■ Are teens being encouraged and given specific, meaningful opportunities to serve in the church?

■ Are the leaders courageously and lovingly addressing unbiblical behavior in the youth group, such as gossip, favoritism, worldliness, impurity, and spiritual apathy?

■ Are family relationships given priority over relationships in the youth group (with leaders and/or peers)? Is this reflected in the youth calendar, or are there so many activities that family priorities suffer?

■ Do the church and youth leaders consult with and solicit the input of parents before counseling teens about specific areas in their lives? If parents don't see or are unwilling to address sinful behavior in their teen, will church leaders lovingly confront them and communicate their concerns?

If you would like more information about how these principles have been applied in our local church, you can request a complimentary copy of the "Fairfax Covenant Church Ministry to Youth" policy by writing to Fairfax Covenant Church, P.O. Box 2279, Fairfax, VA 22031.

The following worksheets by **Wayne A. Mack** *offer parents and teens an in-depth analysis of their relationship. The questions are detailed and probing...don't expect to complete these in one session! But for those eager to act on the principles in this book, we believe you will find these supplemental exercises well worth the effort.*

Worksheet for Parents - No. 1

1. How would you describe your relationship with each of your children? List the name of each child and then describe your relationship as excellent (5), very good (4), good (3), fair (2), poor (1), terrible (0).

2. If you rated your relationships with your child or children as excellent (5), very good (4), or good (3), jot down:

    a. Your reasons for thinking you have a good relationship;

    b. What has hindered a better relationship;

    c. What you might now do to improve your relationship.

3. Put yourself in the place of your children and imagine what you would want from a parent if you were they. What would you want a parent to be? to provide for you? to do for you? Make a list of specific things and then ask if their expectations and desires are reasonable or unreasonable. Are there ways in which you could change without compromising biblical principle to become more the parent your children desire? Circle the ways you could change or improve.

4. List the name of each child and then write down everything you appreciate about each of them. Continue to add to this list. Make it a practice to look for the good qualities, actions, responses, attitudes, conduct, potential in each child. Communicate your appreciation regularly, specifically, and enthusiastically.

5. Make a list of at least 10 fun things that each child enjoys that you can do with him/her. Plan when you will do at least one of these things with your child (children) at least once a week. List all the fun things you did with your child (children) during the last month.

6. How would you describe the communication level of your family? (5) excellent, (4) very good, (3) good, (2) fair, (1) poor, (0) terrible.

7. What are the hindrances to communication on a family level? List them.

8. Is there any person in your family with whom you have the most difficulty communicating? What can you do to break through the communication barrier? How can you improve the communication level of your family?

9. List at least 15 ways that you do or can show love to your children. Think especially in terms of your children's desires, likes, and dislikes. Think in terms of the various aspects of their lives.

Worksheet for Parents - No. 2

1. Consider your parental goals. What qualities do you want to see developed in your children? By the time they are 21 or 22, what kind of persons would you like them to be? What do you hope will have been accomplished? What do you desire they will be prepared to be or do?

2. Compare your goals with the goals that God has for his children. Study the following verses and notice what God wants his children to become. Certainly our goals and his goals should coincide (Matthew 28:19, 20; Exodus 20:1-17; Matthew 22:36-40; Ephesians 4:1-6:20; Romans 12:1-15:7; 1 Corinthians 13; Philippians 2:1-18; 4:1-9; Matthew 5:1-7:27; Luke 6:27-49; Galatians 5:13-6:10).

3. Discuss and write down how you will attempt to assist your children to become and do everything that God wants them to be and do. (Study Philippians 4:9; 2 Timothy 1:5; 3:15-17; Deuteronomy 6:4-9; Hebrews 12:5-11; Proverbs 3:11, 12; 1:8, 9; 22:6, 15, 24, 25; 13:20, 24; 29:15; Ephesians 6:4; 1 Timothy 4:16; 5:8; 1 Corinthians 15:33; Galatians 6:7, 8.)

4. Examine the kind of discipline you are giving to your children. Discuss and write down your answers to the following questions:

   a. What are your children's chores and responsibilities? Do you know? Do they?

   b. What are your disciplinary rules and procedures? Do you know what you expect in specific terms? Do they? Children must know clearly what is expected of them and what will happen if they obey or disobey. Are your expectations realistic and rewards and correction appropriate?

   c. Do you administer discipline consistently and sufficiently?

   d. Do you administer discipline fairly with instruction and love?

   e. Do you impart the idea that you expect obedience and put the prescribed discipline into effect when the child does not immediately obey?

   f. Do you and your mate agree on your expectations and the mechanics of discipline? Don't expect your children to obey or agree or respond to your discipline if you and your mate do not support each other.

   g. Do you really make obedience attractive? Do you think of discipline positively or merely negatively?

5. Study Deuteronomy 6:4-9.

   a. List the parental responsibilities mentioned in this passage.

   b. Discuss how you are fulfilling the parental responsibilities mentioned here. What else could you do?

Worksheet for Teens - No. 1

1. How would you describe your relationship with each of your parents? Describe your relationship as excellent (5), very good (4), good (3), fair (2), poor (1), terrible (0).

2. On a separate sheet of paper, write down:

   a. Your reasons for rating your relationship as you did;

   b. What has helped or hindered your relationship;

   c. What could be done by you to improve your relationship.

3. Put yourself in the place of your parents and imagine what you would want from a child if you were they. What would you want a child to be? to do for you? How would you want your child to respond to you, or to listen to you, to talk to you, to cooperate with you, to communicate and share with you? Make a list and then ask yourself if their expectations are reasonable or unreasonable. Are there ways in which you should change to become a better child? If so, how?

4. Write down the word "father" and then list everything that is good and worthy of respect about him. Think of character traits, attitudes, actions, relationships, activities. Think of every aspect of his life: physical, spiritual, mental, marital, familial, social, verbal, communal, financial, recreational, personal, etc. Continue to add to this list. Make it a practice to look regularly for the good things in your father's life. Communicate your appreciation to him regularly, specifically, and enthusiastically. Do the same thing for your mother.

5. Make a list of at least 10 fun things that each parent enjoys that you can enjoy with him/her. Ask them to do these things with you, and let them know you really want to be with them. Plan to spend time with your parents regularly.

6. How would you describe the communication level of your family? Use the scale listed under question 1.

7. What are the hindrances to your communication with your parents? List them.

8. Is there a parent with whom you have greater difficulty? What can you do to break through the communication barrier with this person? How can you improve the communication level with this person?

9. List at least 15 ways that you do or can show love to your parents. Think especially in terms of your parents' desires, likes, and dislikes. Put the list into practice immediately and continuously.

10. Using the following list as headings, list three items under each heading in order of priority as you think your mother or father would respond: chief joys, disappointments, goals or aspirations, likes, dislikes, interests, concerns, problems.

Worksheet for Teens - No. 2

1. Make a detailed list describing your understanding of a son's or daughter's responsibility to his/her parents. Ask not what should my parents do for me, but what should I do for my parents? What are my responsibilities to them? Be specific and comprehensive. Include the whole sphere of your life and theirs; include your responsibilities in the area of actions, attitudes, time, conversation, sharing, etc.

2. Make a list of the following Scripture verses on a separate sheet of paper and then study each one to determine how God wants you to respond and relate to your parents. Some of the passages deal directly with child-parent relations; others with how we should relate to people in general. These latter passages, of course, are particularly relevant in reference to parents. Scripture (1 Timothy 5:4) says that we should first learn to rightly relate to and care for those of our family. We should learn to rightly relate to all men, but first in order of importance should be the members of our own family. Scripture (1 Timothy 5:4-8) indicates that failure to do so has serious implications.

> Exodus 20:12; Leviticus 19:3; Proverbs 1:8, 9; 4:1; 6:20-22; 11:29; 13:1; 15:20; 17:6, 25; 22:28; 23:22-25; 28:24; 30:17; Romans 1:28-32; 13:1-10; 1 Corinthians 6:1-3; Ephesians 6:1-3; Philippians 2:1-4; Colossians 3:20.

3. In the Bible God gives certain promises to children who obey him in reference to their parents.

    a. List the promises found in the following verses: Exodus 20:12; Proverbs 1:8, 9; 4:1, 2; 6:20-22; Ephesians 6:1-3.

    b. God promises that the child who honors his parents will be blessed—"That it may be well with you" (Ephesians 6:3). Make a list of ways that children who honor their parents are often blessed. (Two suggestions to get started: statistics demonstrate that children who have a good relationship with their parents are much more likely to have happy, fulfilling marriages; they are better adjusted and free to use their emotional and mental energy for constructive purposes—they are not controlled and consumed by resentment and bitterness against and reaction to their parents. This sets them free to really be productive and constructive.)

4. In the Bible God also issues warnings to children who disobey him in reference to their parents.

    a. List the warnings found in the following verses: Proverbs 28:24; 30:17; Romans 1:28-32; 1 Timothy 5:8; Mark 7:8-13; Galatians 6:7.

    b. Think about some of the ways that a son or daughter who dishonors his/her parents may suffer for it. (For example, Galatians 6:7 indicates that he/she should not be surprised if his/her own children relate to him/her exactly as he/she related to his/her parents, only worse.)

Continued...

5. Two words that are frequently used in reference to a child's responsibility to his parents are "obey" and "honor."

  a. Make a list of what your parents expect of you in every aspect of life—at home, school, spiritually, speech, attitudes, dating, etc.

  b. Do you obey your parents in everything? (Colossians 3:20)

  Give two examples of times when you obeyed your parents even though you really did not want to obey.

  Give two examples of times or areas in which you have not or are not obeying them.

  c. Do you honor your parents? (This involves attitude and spirit as well as actions and behavior; when you show disrespect, stubbornness, ingratitude, uncooperativeness, resentment, bitterness, disdain, or contempt, you are not honoring your parents.) Do your parents and others know that you really appreciate and respect them? Examine your attitudes and speech; what you don't do as well as what you do when you answer this question.

  d. Plan at least 10 ways to honor your parents. Begin to put the list into practice immediately.

6. Proverbs 10:1 says that "a wise son [daughter] makes a father glad, but a foolish son [daughter] is a grief to his mother."

  a. List some ways you make your parents glad.

  b. List some things about you that bring them grief.

  c. How could you change to bring them more joy and happiness? Examine your attitudes, speech, behavior, use of money, time, habits, etc.

Worksheets reprinted with permission from *A Homework Manual for Biblical Living,* Vol. 2, by Wayne A. Mack (Presbyterian & Reformed Publishing Company, Box 817, Phillipsburg, NJ, 08865, ©1980).

NOTES FOREWORD

1. George Barna, *The Frog in the Kettle* (Ventura, CA: Regal Books, 1990), p. 21.

STUDY ONE

1. We are indebted to Dr. Michael Platt for the research and insights in his helpful article entitled, "The Myth of the Teenager" in the Summer 1993 issue of *Practical Homeschooling*, pp. 19-21.

2. Platt, "The Myth of the Teenager," p. 20.

3. Michael Keating, "The Stolen Generation," *Pastoral Renewal*, May 1987, pp. 14-15.

4. Michael Keating, "More Than Meets the Ear," *Pastoral Renewal*, July/August 1987, p. 4.

5. George Barna, *The Invisible Generation: Baby Busters* (Glendale, CA: Barna Research Group, Ltd., 1992), p. 17.

6. Ibid., pp. 44, 57, 171.

7. Ian Williams, "Trash That Baby Boom," *The Washington Post Magazine*, January 2, 1994, p. 26.

8. Barna, *The Invisible Generation*, various citings throughout book.

9. David Elkind, *All Grown Up & No Place to Go* (Reading, MA: Addison-Wesley Publishing Company, 1984), p. 9.

10. Barna, *The Invisible Generation*, pp. 167-168.

11. Keating, "The Stolen Generation," p. 12.

12. Fran Sciacca, *Generation at Risk* (Chicago, IL: Moody Press, 1990), p. 172.

STUDY TWO

1. Robert G. DeMoss, Jr., *Learn To Discern* (Grand Rapids, MI: Zondervan Publishing House, 1992), p. 25.

2. Michael Keating, "Highway to Hell," *Pastoral Renewal*, June 1987, p. 5.

3. Oswald Chambers, *My Utmost For His Highest* (New York, NY: Dodd Mead & Co., 1935), p. 173.

4. Dr. Robert Laurent, *Keeping Your Teen In Touch With God* (Elgin, IL: David C. Cook Publishing Co., 1988), p. 35.

5. Keating, "Highway to Hell," p. 4.

6. Thomas a Kempis, *The Imitation of Christ*, translation by Leo Sherley-Price (New York, NY: Penguin Books, 1952), p. 39.

STUDY THREE

1. Sari Horwitz, "Youths Tell Kelly They Want Action," *The Washington Post*, February 3, 1994, B-1, B-3.

2. David Elkind, *All Grown Up & No Place to Go*, p. 13.

3. Gregg Harris, "The Power of Companionship," *People of Destiny* magazine, July/August 1988, p. 16.

4. John Blattner, "Let's Raise Our Children," *Pastoral Renewal*, January 1988, p. 1.

5. Dawson McAllister, interviewed by Ron R. Lee in "What Teens Need Most from Mom & Dad," *Marriage Partnership*, Summer 1993, Vol. 10, No. 3.

6. Dr. Michael Platt, "The Myth of the Teenager," p. 21.

7. Elkind, p. 205.

8. Blattner, p. 10.

9. Dr. Robert Laurent, *Keeping Your Teen In Touch With God*, pp. 125-6.

STUDY FOUR

1. David Elkind, *All Grown Up & No Place to Go*, p. 201.
2. John Blattner, "Let's Raise Our Children," p. 11.
3. Gordon MacDonald, *The Effective Father* (Wheaton, IL: Tyndale House Publishers, 1977), p. 40.
4. Michael Keating, "The Stolen Generation," p. 14.
5. Elkind, p. 100.
6. Elkind, p. 4.
7. Robert G. DeMoss, Jr., *Learn To Discern*, p. 169.
8. Henri Frederic Amiel, quoted in *3000 Quotations on Christian Themes* by Carroll E. Simcox (Grand Rapids, MI: Baker Book House, 1988), p. 55.
9. Fran Sciacca, *Generation At Risk*, pp. 221-222.

STUDY FIVE

1. G.K. Chesterton, quoted in *Bartlett's Familiar Quotations, 15th Edition* (Boston, MA: Little, Brown and Company, 1980), p. 742.
2. John Blattner, "Let's Raise Our Children," p. 11.
3. J.C. Ryle, *Thoughts For Young Men* (Amityville, NY: Calvary Press, 1993; revised from 1886 edition by Wm. Hunt & Co., London), p. 39.
4. David Elkind, *All Grown Up & No Place to Go*, p. 171.
5. Michael Keating, "Highway to Hell," p. 6.
6. Jerry White, *The Power of Commitment* (Colorado Springs, CO: NavPress, 1985), p. 67.
7. Dr. Robert Laurent, *Keeping Your Teen In Touch With God*, preface.
8. Charles Colson and Ellen Santilli Vaughn, *The Body* (Dallas, TX: Word, Inc., 1992), p. 70.
9. John of the Cross, quoted in *3000 Quotations on Christian Themes*, p. 82.

STUDY SIX

1. Joshua Harris, "Dating Problems, Courtship Solutions," *New Attitude Magazine*, Vol. 1, No. 2.
2. Ellen K. Rothman, *Hands and Hearts: A History of Courtship in America* (New York, NY: Basic Books Inc., 1984), pp. 39-40.
3. Samuel Hopkins (1765), from *The Life and Character of the Late Reverend Mr. Jonathan Edwards*, quoted in *Christian History*, Issue 8.
4. Most of our information on the history of dating was taken from *Hands and Hearts: A History of Courtship in America* by Ellen K. Rothman.
5. Jim West, *Christian Courtship vs. the Dating Game* (Palo Cedro, CA: Christian Worldview Ministries, 1993), p. 34.
6. John Holzmann, *Dating With Integrity* (Brentwood, TN: Wolgemuth & Hyatt Publishers, 1990), p. 223.
7. Michael P. Farris, *The Homeschooling Father* (Hamilton, VA: Michael P. Farris, 1992), p. 65.
8. Harris, "Dating Problems, Courtship Solutions."
9. Quoted in Harris, "Dating Problems, Courtship Solutions."
10. We're indebted to Joshua Harris for letting us adapt this list, which originally appeared in *New Attitude Magazine*, Vol. 1, No. 2. Josh launched this magazine for home-schooling teens at age 18, and is doing a tremendous job with it!)
11. Connie Marshner, *Decent Exposure: How to Teach Your Children about Sex* (Brentwood, TN: Wolgemuth & Hyatt Publishers, 1988), p. 167.

STUDY SEVEN

1. George Barna, *The Invisible Generation*, pp. 142, 145.
2. Fran Sciacca, *Generation At Risk*, p. 158.
3. J.C. Ryle, *Thoughts For Young Men*, p. 10.
4. Elisabeth Elliot, *Passion and Purity* (Old Tappan, NJ: Fleming H. Revell Company, 1984), pp. 131-32.
5. Quoted in Josh McDowell and Dick Day, *Why Wait?* (San Bernardino, CA: Here's Life Publishers, 1987), p. 15.
6. Elliot, p. 124.
7. John Holzmann, *Dating With Integrity*, p.126.
8. Quoted by J.C. Ryle in *Thoughts For Young Men*, p. 11.
9. Burdette Palmberg, "Private Sins of Public Ministry," *Leadership*, Winter 1988, p. 20.
10. Connie Marshner, *Decent Exposure*, p. 106.

STUDY EIGHT

1. Dallas Willard, *The Spirit of the Disciplines* (San Francisco, CA: HarperCollins Publishers, 1991), pp. 3-4.
2. J.C. Ryle, *Thoughts For Young Men*, p. 70.
3. Jerry Bridges, *The Practice of Godliness* (Colorado Springs, CO: NavPress, 1983), p. 75.
4. Jay Adams, *The Christian Counselor's Manual* (Grand Rapids, MI: Zondervan Publishing House, 1973), p. 118.
5. Jerry Bridges, *The Pursuit of Holiness* (Colorado Springs, CO: NavPress, 1978), p. 84.
6. Oswald Chambers, *My Utmost For His Highest*, p. 141.
7. John Blattner, "Let's Raise Our Children," p. 12.
8. C.J. Mahaney and John Loftness, *Disciplined For Life* (Gaithersburg, MD: People of Destiny International, 1992), pp. 96, 97.

STUDY NINE

1. Quoted by Dawson McAllister in "What Teens Need Most from Mom & Dad," p. 30.
2. John Piper, *The Pleasures of God* (Portland, OR: Multnomah Press, 1991), p. 252.
3. F.F. Bruce, *The Letter of Paul To The Romans: An Introduction and Commentary* (Grand Rapids, MI: Eerdmans Publishing Co., 1985), pp. 129-130.
4. Jay Kesler, from the foreword to *Keeping Your Teen In Touch With God*, by Dr. Robert Laurent.
5. J.C. Ryle, *Thoughts For Young Men*, p. 14.
6. Jay Kesler, *Raising Responsible Kids* (Brentwood, TN: Wolgemuth & Hyatt Publishers, 1991), p. 64.
7. Dr. Robert Laurent, *Keeping Your Teen In Touch With God,* p. 49.

STUDY TEN

1. Jonathan Edwards, *Representative Selections, with Introduction, Bibliography, and Notes*, Clarence H. Faust and Thomas H. Johnson, ed. (New York, NY: Hill and Wang, revised edition, 1962), p. 38.
2. Charles Spurgeon, *The Treasury of David, Vol. II* (Peabody, MA: Hendrickson Publishers), p. 65.
3. J.C. Ryle, *Thoughts For Young Men*, p. 7.
4. Oswald Chambers, *My Utmost For His Highest*, p. 335.
5. Ryle, p. 13.
6. Dr. Robert Laurent, *Keeping Your Teen In Touch With God*, preface.
7. Fran Sciacca, *Generation at Risk*, p. 159.
8. Dawson McAllister, "What Teens Need Most from Mom & Dad."

OTHER TITLES IN THIS SERIES

Disciplined For Life   C.J. Mahaney and John Loftness
Are you satisfied with the depth of your devotional life? If you're like most Christians, probably not.

Disciplined For Life puts change within your grasp. Leave the treadmill of spiritual drudgery behind as you discover fresh motivation and renewed passion to practice the spiritual disciplines. (112 pages)

This Great Salvation   C.J. Mahaney and Robin Boisvert
Like a pair of heavyweight boxers, Accusation and Condemnation hit us with guilt. Confusion. Doubt. You may even be "in the ring" with them now.

But you don't have to take it! Nothing combats legalism and false guilt like the truth of justification. As you study the amazing implications of Christ's work on the cross, this book will teach you how to fight back. (112 pages)

Love That Lasts   Gary and Betsy Ricucci
A magnificent marriage is more than wishful thinking. It can and should be the experience of every husband and wife willing to follow God's plan for them as a couple.

Whether your marriage is new, needy, or simply ready for a refresher, here is an excellent guide for helping you build a thriving, lasting love. (176 pages)

From Glory To Glory   C.J. Mahaney and Robin Boisvert
From Glory To Glory rests on a remarkable assumption: If you will study and apply the doctrine of sanctification, any sin can be overcome.

Have you known the frustration of falling short in your efforts to please God? Have you questioned whether you will *ever* be able to change? If so, this book will have a profound impact on your walk with Christ. (112 pages)

In addition to study books, People of Destiny International publishes a number of other resources to equip the church for action:

Worship Tapes: Contemporary, upbeat music with penetrating lyrics.

Testimony Tapes: Dramatic stories of God's power to deliver and restore. Each tape addresses a specific theme (such as "Marriage In Crisis" and "Tragedy") and includes a brief gospel message—perfect for evangelistic giveaway!

Teaching Tapes: Messages on raising teens, biblical masculinity, leadership issues, and many more.

People of Destiny Magazine: In circulation for over a decade, this bimonthly publication addresses the most critical issues facing Christians today. It also profiles the people and progress of People of Destiny's related churches in the United States and abroad.

For a catalog and a free issue of *People of Destiny*, call **1-800-736-2202** or write to:

People of Destiny International
7881 Beechcraft Avenue, Suite B
Gaithersburg, MD 20879
Attention: Resource Center